THE GLORY IN YOUR STORY

THE GLORY IN YOUR STORY

ACTIVATING *a* FEARLESS FAITH
to CHANGE YOUR LIFE,
Your CAREER, *and the* WORLD

BY MONIQUE RODRIGUEZ
WITH TRACEY M. LEWIS-GIGGETTS

W PUBLISHING GROUP

AN IMPRINT OF THOMAS NELSON

Published in Nashville, Tennessee, by W Publishing, an imprint of Thomas Nelson. W Publishing and Thomas Nelson are registered trademarks of HarperCollins Christian Publishing, Inc.

Published in association with United Talent Agency.

Thomas Nelson titles may be purchased in bulk for educational, business, fundraising, or sales promotional use. For information, please email SpecialMarkets@ThomasNelson.com.

ISBN 978-1-4003-4983-8 (hardcover)
ISBN 978-1-4003-4985-2 (audiobook)
ISBN 978-1-4003-4984-5 (ePub)

Library of Congress Control Number: 2024949154

Printed in the United States of America
25 26 27 28 29 LBC 5 4 3 2 1

For Milan

Contents

Introduction

Seek God First

THE START OF THE NEW MILLENNIUM SAW INCREDIBLE shifts across every aspect of life and industry. As we put away our Y2K fears, we were oblivious to the fact that we were only a few months away from the bursting of the dot-com bubble. It was an election year and ramping up to be a contentious season of debates. Aaliyah was on my radio telling me to "dust myself off and try again," and OutKast was teaching the importance of being "so fresh and so clean."

And on the streets of Chicago's South Side, where there'd long been a bustling community of Black folks making ways out of no way, a seventeen-year-old girl was experiencing her own shifts, though mostly internal. She was beautiful and brilliant—I can see that now—and she had a deep longing for more. God was giving her a vision that would not be fully formed for many years, but the seeds were being planted and the harvest would come.

If I could go back in time and speak to teenage Monique—the girl from the South Side thinking about being a nurse, but who, deep down, longed for more—there is so much I would say to her. Isn't that usually how it goes? Hindsight is 20/20, as they say.

Though young Monique couldn't even have begun to dream of the life she has now, still I'd tell her to keep the faith. As I think about all she went through, I wish I could weave the thread of faith into every fiber of her being, because I know it is her faith that would move mountains and turn her dreams into reality. There would certainly be days and months and years that would feel long and arduous. There absolutely would be times when the sorrow and loss felt never-ending. And yet, as long as she sought God, grief would not overtake her.

She didn't know it, but in less than a decade she would experience one of the greatest tragedies of her life—the loss of her only son. Everything would go dark, it would seem as if the ground had fallen out from beneath her, she would grow angry, and her heart would feel like it had been broken into a million pieces. Gratefully, it was in those dark days that she found her way to God and the church. Mostly because she needed something—anything—to hold on to. Something—*Someone*—bigger than herself. When she laid her burdens down and surrendered to God, she found a strength she never knew she had.

There is beauty in surrendering our vision to God's plan. It requires trusting Him to order our footsteps. It is a journey of faith, of relinquishing control and embracing the mystery of God's design. The vision we have might not be normal. It might not be status quo. It might not even be something we or anyone else has seen before. But that's okay. There's something wonderful on the other side of our leap of faith.

Mielle Organics, a Black hair care company I founded with Melvin in 2014, was just a seed of an idea during this time. Now it's one of the most successful Black-owned hair companies in the world. Ironically, the business was *birthed* fully in the aftermath of loss. During the months prior to its launch, I awakened every day with grief that felt like a weight on my chest. But every day I also awakened to my two beautiful little girls, Mia and Mackenzie, whom I did not want to see me fall apart. On the days I couldn't press on for myself, God helped me press on for them. On the inside I felt like I was breaking, for sure. But on the outside? I held it together and began to plant that seed into fertile ground. I believe God honored that persistence, and over a decade later I'm living in the fruit of it.

———

What I would tell young Monique might be what you would tell younger you: Believe in the gifts God has given you. Take that first step, even though you can't see where the path is taking you. Do not hesitate to leap. Because let's be completely real! We certainly serve a God who has no limits, but when we start second-guessing His vision for our lives, we end up holding back the floodgates of blessings waiting to pour into us.

I think I would also tell young Monique to be wary of pride. It is a treacherous companion. It is way too easy to find your stride and think that you somehow did it all yourself. Or that you don't need help. Inevitably, life will show you otherwise. The world of business certainly will. Whenever I've acknowledged my limitations and sought good counsel, I've always seen success. I have not accomplished what I have alone. There are so many Black women entrepreneurs who have come before me, many of whose names I will mention throughout this book.

I also want you to see that your success is not just the fruit of your own labor but the outcome of others'. As you carry the dreams of those who came before you, do everything in your power to blaze a trail for those yet to come. The journey we travel in life is not defined by the destination but by the lives we touch along the way. That's how we become what famed journalist and activist Maria Shriver calls "architects of change."[1]

Finally, I would wholeheartedly tell young Monique to believe only the report of the Lord. There will be people who don't get it. Who won't get her. Those who don't know her heart and won't dare ask her intentions because that might destroy their preconceived notions of who she is. "Oh, sweet girl," I'd say, "keep going anyway."

Starting a business is no joke. Growing a business to the level we have is even less so. People will doubt you, criticize you, maybe even hate on you. Sometimes those people will look like you. And I get it. Black folks in particular are protective of the things we've built. We've had to be. I say "we" because we are a culture that often has a collective mindset. When one of us wins, we all win. And that is a very good thing. But we've also watched our culture be commodified repeatedly with no regard for the impact on our communities. So any talk of "selling" one of our own is understandably painful. But I firmly believe that it doesn't have to be either/or. It can be both/and. And on these pages, I want to talk about how we accomplish that.

In this regard, I think I would further tell young Monique that no, it will never feel good to know that there are those who will *not* cheer for entrepreneurs who look like them, that when one of their own dares to carve a path, they will have nothing but negativity to offer. But Mavens and Mavericks, do not make the haters your focus. I've discovered that the journey I am on is not just about building empires but dismantling barriers. It's about rewriting narratives that have long confined Black people—Black women in particular—to the margins of business.

When chasing a dream, it does no good to worry about those who don't get it. I simply have to do as Proverbs 3:5–6 says: "Trust in the LORD with all your heart and lean not on your own understanding; in all your ways submit to him, and he will make your paths straight." Each negotiation, each strategic decision is a testament to my faith in God and my resilience in the face of overwhelming odds. I encourage you to see any obstacle as an opportunity. It's in the tension of growth that we learn what we are made of and can use that to win.

There's a saying that goes, "What you focus on grows." So can we focus on growing the positive and leaving the negative behind? Yes, there will be bumps in the road and storms that surround us. When we pursue purpose, challenges will come from every direction. In these pages, I will share some of the storms I've lived through—and still encounter regularly. But having a solid foundation is what matters, and you, too, can weather anything when you are rooted in faith and integrity.

There are two stories being revealed in these pages. The story of Monique—the girl, the woman, the wife, the mother—and the story of Mielle Organics, the multimillion-dollar empire built by that woman. At times, these stories will be distinct. Different. Not yet fused together. Sometimes even intentionally so. At some point, however, these stories will converge, as they often do for entrepreneurs. There are times when my personal life is nearly indistinguishable from my professional life. In either case, I hope the outcome provides you with a powerful set of core principles that can help you as you envision a better life for yourself.

Every twist and turn on my journey has led me here. To this life. To these blessings. To writing this book. The grief, the struggles, the moments of doubt—they all shaped me. They are responsible for the nuggets of wisdom I hope to share with you. Even as I look ahead, I know there are more challenges waiting for me. Yet, armed with faith and a heart full of gratitude, I'm ready to take them on. I hope that by the end, you will say the same. As Luke 1:37 says, "With God nothing will be impossible" (NKJV).

Each chapter of this book is anchored with a core principle I've learned from life and business. I will share with you not only the story of how I arrived at each principle but also how you might use it to live the most purpose-filled life you can. Whether you are an aspiring entrepreneur or someone who is just trying to figure out life and needs some inspiration, I deeply desire for you to feel a kinship with young Monique from the South Side of Chicago who once walked in your proverbial shoes. I want you to know that I'm no different from you, and if I could rise above the challenges that threatened to drown me, then surely you can too.

By the time you turn the last page, I want you to know this fundamental truth I have learned: Faith is the cornerstone of every victory. God can breathe life into every vision you've had, every dream you've written down. He wants to be your ever-present guide, as He has been for me. It's time, my friend, to get out of your own way and let God lead you to a destiny beyond your wildest imagination.

—Monique

Finding True North on the South Side

Guiding Principle:
Embrace the path God has given you.

AS A LITTLE GIRL, I WAS OBSESSED WITH ALL THINGS beauty. I was fascinated by that world and constantly bugged my mom to enter me into local and regional beauty pageants. From an early age, I'd walk through Jewel grocery store with my mother and make my way to the beauty aisle. I was especially dazzled by the pictures of little girls with curly ponytails or bone-straight hair and big white smiles on the front of the Just for Me relaxer kits. It was one of the only places I saw little girls who looked like me.

"I want to do that," I'd say to my mother, pointing to the colorful box.

My mother was all about supporting my dreams—as long as those dreams made sense to her. She didn't know anyone in the modeling industry, so she had no point of reference other than what was on television. She took me to exactly one pageant after I begged her to and had gone online to sign up for it myself. Mom couldn't see a stable future in any of it and

1

soon became resistant to the idea entirely, despite my pressing the point. After years of no progress, no pageant wins, and no modeling contracts, reality hit hard, and she finally drew the line.

"This costs money I really don't have, Monique. It's best you just go to school. I'm going to teach you how to survive."

And that was it. No auditions, runways, or photo shoots for me. Not yet anyway.

As a teenager, while some of my friends were still hopeful that their dreams could come true, I had to shift my thoughts to more practical aspirations. Mostly because there was no one else around to show me—or my mother—that anything different was possible. Kids can't be what they don't see, and I didn't see beauty moguls on my block. I didn't know anyone who made their own products and sold enough to make a living at it. What I *did* see were women who looked like me working sensible jobs and making "good enough" money. They could pay their bills, get their hair done, tithe to the church or the club—depending on which way they leaned—and do their absolute best to provide some kind of stable foundation for their children. As far as I could see, and according to my mother, the people in our community who didn't seem to struggle financially were the ones who held respectable jobs in hospitals, schools, or the government. And that was fine. Just fine. As I said, none of them, nor me at the time, could dream of running a multimillion-dollar business. There wasn't much room for wanting more. There was certainly no room for a vision of global proportions. So I obeyed my mother and put my childhood dreams away.

To be fair, it wasn't like Mom didn't know what she was talking about. I'm sure she believed she was doing the right thing. Mom was a unit secretary at the University of Chicago Hospital for over forty years. She was acutely aware that nursing was one of the few recession-proof careers out there. She wanted that for me because she wanted me to be safe and cared for. So she introduced me to her nurse friends, and I saw for myself how they were living. They had much nicer cars compared to the used one we had. Their homes were huge compared to our small house. My mom was always struggling to provide, often barely making ends meet, so there was a big difference between the back-to-school clothes her friends' kids wore from Marshall Field's and the clothes she bought off the clearance racks at T.J. Maxx. The unintentional consequence of my seeing all this was that I quickly believed my dreams were unachievable and unrealistic, so I pursued someone else's.

Well, I want what they have, so this is what I should do when I grow up, I thought.

So I went to nursing school, got my degree at twenty-two, and landed a job in a hospital. I stayed there for eight and a half years tending to patients, clocking in and out, and living a life that seemed perfectly fine. But every now and then, whenever I'd stop moving a mile a minute, when the noise in my head got really quiet and I chose to listen to the rumblings deep down in my heart, there was always this nagging feeling, this sense that I was meant for something more.

A few years into my career as a nurse, I gravitated toward the high-risk wards in hospitals. It wasn't just the adrenaline that drew me in; it was the opportunity to learn and grow. And I did. I learned how to care for patients in some of the most vulnerable and heartbreaking situations. I witnessed maternal-fetal deaths and teenage pregnancies born of molestation, and I even cared for a thirteen-year-old rape victim who was pregnant. These experiences shaped me in ways I couldn't have anticipated. They taught me empathy—not just as a nurse but as a person. I learned to connect with people from every walk of life and to treat them with dignity and fairness, no matter their race, age, or background. I also learned how to not only do my job but manage up. (Working with doctors and administrators will absolutely test your patience.)

That foundation of empathy stayed with me, even as I transitioned into entrepreneurship. It's what I poured into Mielle Organics. The same commitment to understanding people's needs—whether they are patients or customers—is at the heart of what I do.

Please know there was and is nothing wrong with being a nurse. But I felt deep in my bones that I was called to do something else. Nevertheless, I also know God used every experience I had in the health-care field for my good. In fact, that medical background played a huge role in my personal life. It may have even saved my life. When I went into labor with my son, I quickly realized I wasn't getting the level of care I knew I deserved. It was a sobering realization, amplified by my knowledge of what should have been happening. There were, for sure, times when knowing too much felt like a curse. I understood medical jargon, and I could explain it to my husband, but it also meant I recognized every warning sign in real time. Balancing that knowledge with faith was one of the hardest things I've ever done—leaning on God while navigating the harsh realities of what I knew. That tension, though, made me stronger.

———

After losing my baby boy, which I'll share more about later, and spending months in a fog of grief and despair, I slowly emerged from that headspace with the realization that I could not return to my previous life. I'd grown to love my career in nursing, but my season was changing and there was something else God had for me. I could have ignored that feeling. I could have decided to return to what was safe and familiar. But God had shown Himself faithful to me during one of the most painful periods of my life, so I was not going to turn my back on what I was hearing. I leaned in to that still small voice pulling me toward something else. The dreams that lay dormant in me began to show up, and this time I chose to listen to them. It was time to reclaim my agency. To refuse to settle for a life that didn't fulfill me. It was time to show the world—and myself— that anything is possible with God.

Even before our loss, Melvin and I had cycled through numerous business ideas. We did just about everything, starting with direct sales. Multilevel marketing was sold to us as a get-rich-quick path to success, so we started with a cable company called ACN. Eventually, I realized selling cable didn't excite me, so I switched to something I loved—beauty. I first became a Mary Kay representative, then switched to Avon. I hosted parties and stocked inventory but barely sold anything. Next, I tried Scentsy candles, but the story was the same. Realizing direct sales—at least in the way I was introduced to it—wasn't for me, I launched a jewelry business, selling pieces out of my car and on Facebook. Despite initial sales, that venture fizzled too. Thankfully, I didn't give up. Each failure taught me resilience, and I'm incredibly grateful for that.

After a few more false starts, and in the midst of great pain and grief, I finally started exploring the idea that I could create hair products that were safer and more effective for textured hair like my own.

I spent countless hours researching and experimenting with ingredients and oils. I put myself out there on social media as I tested the products on my own hair. There were so many late nights when the only things fueling me were passion and determination. Were there also days when I wanted to give up? When doubt and fear threatened to consume me? When the Enemy whispered in my ear, *Who do you think you are? Ain't you just a little girl from the South Side? Who told you that you can create something?* Sure. But I refused to let go of the promise of God that said, "I can do all things through Christ who strengthens me" (Philippians 4:13 NKJV).

Clearly that persistence, that belief in God and myself, paid off. I would not be writing this book if it hadn't. But I will not pretend that the road was not long and arduous. Each time I felt like giving up, I reminded myself of the little girl walking the aisles of the grocery store, dreaming of gracing the covers of magazines and perm boxes. The teenager who drove through neighborhoods lined with mansions and fancy cars with her boyfriend/future husband and longed for a bigger life but didn't know how to obtain it.

And I kept going.

This first principle of embracing the path God has given you is a profound one. It's a starting point. A foundational truth. Never let anyone else dictate your dreams. Listen to your heart, trust your instincts, and never be afraid to chase after what sets your soul on fire. That feeling in your gut? That dream in your heart? That plan in your head? God has placed it there for a reason. It doesn't mean that the journey will be easy. It takes courage to do something different from what you've seen. Your roots can certainly anchor you, which is not necessarily a bad thing, but you have to nurture that seed God gave you. You must water it. Feed it. That way, when you bloom, you will stretch toward the sun and be a glorious manifestation of God's grace and favor.

Never let anyone else dictate your dreams.

I will never forget where I came from. I am grateful for the way my mom taught me how to survive. How she worked to keep me safe. I'm thankful for the ways my early experiences shaped and formed me into the woman I am today. I am the embodiment of Romans 8:28: "All things work together for good to those who love God, to those who are the called according to His purpose" (NKJV). The beauty of that is, I get to tell you that a different path, one greater than you could ever imagine, is available for you if you are willing to embrace it. If you are willing to quiet the noise of all the other voices and follow the vision God has given you, the path He has laid out. Poet Maya Angelou wrote, "If you're always trying to be normal, you will never know how amazing you can be."[1] Tap into your amazing and don't let go. Even—and maybe especially—when life is challenging.

QUESTIONS FOR REFLECTION

- Consider the journey you've taken so far. In what ways has God used experiences, even those that were painful or unexpected, to prepare you for your current path? How can you nurture this connection to move forward with purpose and confidence?

- How do you handle moments of doubt or fear when pursuing a goal that feels bigger than yourself? What spiritual practices or affirmations can help you remain steadfast and connected to your faith, especially when challenges arise?

Who You Are Is More Than What You've Seen

2

Guiding Principle:
See beyond your circumstances.

MY FATHER IS A LOVING MAN. FULL STOP.

What is also true: My father's battle with addiction often over-shadowed the good traits others should have seen and experienced from him. There were plenty of times growing up when my days were filled with laughter and warmth. However, these were too often interspersed with nights of uncertainty and even fear. That tension, that paradox, colored my early childhood years and for the longest time influenced how I saw the world.

To be clear, none of that has stopped me from being successful. In the same way, your past—whatever it might look like—doesn't have to stop you. Our circumstances, good or bad, do not determine our destiny. *We* do. So don't dismiss the underdog or discount someone because of their

Our circumstances, good or bad, do not determine our destiny.

upbringing or even their current situation. No one should ever look at a kid and say, "Oh, because of where you come from, you won't be able to do _____." But it happens all the time. People project what someone's future should be, forgetting that with God, *all* things are possible. There are plenty of stories of people who have overcome even when society or those around them never thought it possible. In fact, I am one of those people.

In today's culture, there's often a prevailing idea that in order to see any success that's not handed down to you through generational wealth, you must somehow find the strength to pull yourself up by your bootstraps. It's a concept that resonates for people differently depending on their background. For those of us who grew up in environments marked by hardship and scarcity, the notion of simply pulling oneself up feels insurmountable and often doesn't account for the very real systemic obstacles one has to overcome. It then becomes too easy to listen to those negative voices and allow your environment to dictate your destiny.

I have a different perspective, though. This idea of pulling yourself up by your bootstraps only offers half of the instructions needed for true success—the kind that doesn't exhaust you or turn sour after several years. Yes, it's important to push yourself to do your absolute best no matter where you came from. Beyond that, though, I'm a witness that putting faith in the One, true living God—trusting that He will order your steps—will extend your capacity in ways you can't even imagine.

It's this second part that people often miss.

The bootstrap theory implies that you can do everything on your own. That succeeding in life and business requires your own strength and nothing more. But that has not been my experience at all. While I've certainly prioritized learning and growing and doing the work, there is no doubt in my mind that God orchestrated and transformed all those things that were completely out of my control—including the hardships of my upbringing—for my good and for His purposes.

———

Some of my earliest memories of my father are from when I was five or six years old, sitting in the back seat of our old family car as he drove around our South Side Chicago neighborhood. One of our favorite things to do was go to the annual Bud Billiken Parade, historically the second-largest parade in the country next to the Rose Parade.[1] Bud Billiken has been a yearly celebration of youth, education, and African American life in Chicago since 1929.

One trip to the parade started off as a wonderful father-daughter moment. I sat on Dad's broad shoulders so I could get the best view of the bands and floats as they moved down the street. We ate turkey legs and cotton candy, and laughed so much together that day. That is, until he got into a terrible fight. Then he became someone else. As the confrontation intensified, Dad tossed me off his shoulders and started beating the man right in front of me. I sat there stunned and crying, feeling helpless as always. When Mom found out what happened, she was livid.

"So we fighting people in the streets now?"

In hindsight, that experience seems like a metaphor for the back-and-forth, up-and-down roller coaster that marked my entire childhood. I absolutely knew joy; there is no doubt about that. But something always felt off. Different. Uncertain. As I said at the opening of this chapter, my dad has a good heart, and he's usually mild-mannered, calm, and laid back. A very good person with a very bad disease. I'm thankful every day that his addiction didn't turn him into some mean, abusive person as addicts are often stereotyped. Sure, that's possible when you relinquish control of your mind to a substance. But my father was none of that. Reckless? Certainly. Evil? No. Regardless of what he did when he was gone, he still came home and did his best.

I never saw my father using in front of me, though there would be remnants of his activities—an ashtray here, a bottle there. On occasion we'd find him nodding off, and while we knew he was high, it often looked like he was just sleeping or very tired. My younger brother and I mostly just saw Dad begging my mom for money every time she got paid.

Or we'd hear Mom fussing at him because he could never keep a job. As soon as Dad made any progress, he'd do something to get fired. He also went through cars like hotcakes. To the point where she'd hide her car keys in case he got the notion to take (read: sell) hers.

As a child, I often felt like I was living two lives. On the outside, I was a friendly, albeit introverted kid who loved school and excelled at most things I put my mind to. But on the inside, I was constantly grappling with the chaos at home. One of the most challenging aspects of growing up with an addicted parent is the unpredictability. You never know what to expect, and that uncertainty can be incredibly destabilizing.

I was around five or six when I first noticed something was off. Dad had a laissez-faire attitude when it came to most responsibilities, which seemed, even to my young self, reflective of something deeper going on. For instance, because my mother left for work very early, my father was responsible for taking me to school. Sadly, this was a duty he often failed to fulfill. Dad worked nights, so the plan was for him to get me to school before he came home to rest from his shift. He didn't always do that. There were way too many days when he'd oversleep because he'd gone to get high after work. This meant that by the time he needed to get me ready for school, he was passed out on the bed. On those days, I spent my time in front of the television watching cartoons or game shows.

I think part of the reason why he felt okay with doing this is because I was basically a good kid. Even at five years old, Dad trusted that I wasn't going to get into anything. I wasn't going to burn the house down or run around outside. But what he maybe didn't consider is that I was also a very smart and intuitive kid. One who, unfortunately, thought of her dad as more of a big brother. A big brother who she'd absolutely, positively snitch on. I *always* ended up telling my mom when Dad didn't take me to school, or pretty much anything else he did wrong. And of course, my mother would get so upset when she found out.

"Why didn't you take her to school?"

A blank stare was his typical response.

Dad, to me, later: "You run your mouth too much."

I guess.

I just didn't know what else to do. And I wasn't supposed to know. Even at such a young age, I knew that something wasn't right with this dynamic in our household. Whenever I heard my parents argue about why I wasn't going to school, I imagine my little mind was thinking some version of, *Why do I have to tell on this grown man who is supposed to be my dad? Isn't he supposed to be the one looking out for me?*

I felt this same kind of tension when it came to our "fun" rides around the city. A huge part of me was glad to spend one-on-one time with my dad. But another part of me understood that some of the places we were going and the people we'd pick up along the way were not what I should have been exposed to at such a young age. There were even times when he'd bring me around his drug addict friends, some of whom were pimps and prostitutes.

It's only by the grace of God that, for the most part, no one bothered me.

The interesting thing is that I wasn't scared. I never felt fear in the presence of my father. It was more like a deep, unsettling sense that something was profoundly wrong. I was also never really afraid to be in these places or around people who were so different from me. At the end of the day, I was a very friendly kid. To me, having a conversation with a prostitute was the same as having a conversation with anyone else. I held no judgment.

On one of our trips, Dad picked me up from the Catholic school I attended. I was dressed neatly in one of the only two uniforms I had, and my dad knew how angry Mom would be if I got it dirty. So after picking me up, he took me into this alley next to a dilapidated garage and told me to "just go in there and change." *There* happened to be through an old, rusted door that led to one of the dark, unused bays of the garage.

I was six.

Thinking about that now, as a mom, in a world where sex trafficking is common, I get chills. Anything could have happened to me. But of course, Dad wasn't in his right mind. All he could think about at that moment was how to hurry me up so he could take me wherever he needed and then go find his next high.

I honestly think my mom was in a little bit of denial. She wanted to believe my dad wouldn't do anything *too* stupid. Even with the drugs. I suspect this was because she knew a side of him that my brother and I didn't. A caring and compassionate side. A responsible, cautious side. A side that didn't really exist when he was high. Plus, somebody had to work. Somebody had to pay the bills. There was nothing she could do but trust and pray that everything would turn out okay, even if she wasn't sure it would.

———

Dad might have been the one who took us to parades and fun car rides around the city, but Mom was the stable one. The one who made the security of our household a priority. That had always been their dynamic. So while I was challenged by the ups and downs caused by my father, I found comfort in the orderly world of my mother, who worked hard to provide for us in the midst of it all. Mom was determined to create a sense of normalcy for us. She pushed education as the ticket to a better life.

I believe this is also why my mother made the choice to not talk about what my father was dealing with. Addiction was something we never, ever discussed. But it was always the elephant in the room. A topic we skirted around, brushing it aside as though acknowledging it out loud would somehow make it worse.

When my brother, who is five years younger than me, came along, I'm sure my mother hoped things would get better. They didn't. There were times when Dad would take my brother, like he did with me, on his notorious rides. He'd drive around with his barely one-year-old baby boy for hours with no way for my mother to get in contact with him. I remember this mostly happening when the rent was due and he'd just gotten paid. On those days, he'd disappear. It was common for me and Mom to get in her car and drive around the whole South Side looking for him. Thankfully, she always seemed to know where to find him.

One time, we pulled up to my dad's car on some random street and found my brother in the back seat with some other addicts. It was one of the first times I saw my mother completely lose it. She went into a rage and pulled her baby out of the car. They argued for a good while before Mom finally took us both back home.

———

As a child, I tried to make sense of everything in my own way. When I was ten, I took some flour from one of the containers that sat on our kitchen counter and laid it out. Where I'm from, everyone had an idea of what drugs looked like, and if we didn't, we had images on television to tell us. And since I was such an intuitive kid, I figured things out pretty quickly. So after putting the flour out, I took some straws that I'd cut up and laid them next to the flour.

"Ma, come look! Come look at this! What is *that*?" I said as I pointed to the white powder sprinkled all around.

In my ten-year-old mind, I just wanted to see her reaction. I wanted her to say, "I know Mickey didn't leave this stuff in this house." I *needed* her to say the thing she wouldn't say. To answer the questions I had in my head. Was my dad really on drugs or not?

Of course, my mama is nobody's fool. She quickly figured out it was flour. She shook her head and looked at me, but she didn't say a word. She didn't—couldn't—give me the reaction I desperately wanted. She just cleaned up my mess and threw everything in the garbage.

I think Mom didn't name what was going on because she didn't think we were mature enough to really understand it. That's probably why she was very intentional about always keeping us busy. And I suppose by the time we were old enough to figure it all out, she didn't think she needed to explain it. By then, her casual instructions to us were enough to clue us in.

"Don't leave your money lying around the house," she'd say.

"Hide all of your jewelry," she'd remind me.

As a child, I couldn't wrap my mind around why Mom didn't talk about the addiction more. But now, as a mother, I think I understand. This is how she chose to survive. How she made it through. She wouldn't allow herself to break down in front of me and my brother. She was a fiercely resilient woman, the breadwinner, the unwavering pillar of stability in our household, and as such, she had to keep our family's struggles close to her chest. She focused on working to provide for us and filling our lives with as much love and stability as she could muster.

I've often wondered why Mom stayed, and I think there are myriad reasons. I imagine there was a time when she loved Dad deeply. And I'm sure she hoped and wanted to see him turn things around. Every time he came home clean from rehab, I could see a little bit of her softness show up. But I suppose after multiple stints, it got to the point where she couldn't even trust that.

But mostly, my mom is old school. She wanted her children to have a two-parent household. She had no desire to introduce another man to her children—especially raising a little girl. In her mind, it was better for her to stay with her husband for the sake of her kids, no matter what was going on. She was willing to accept the devil she knew as opposed to the one she didn't. And I get it. There has always been a stigma put on Black families that are led by single, Black women. This was even more prevalent in the 1980s and '90s. Mom did not want to feed into any of the prevailing stereotypes, and she certainly didn't want those stereotypes to influence my and my brother's ability to be successful. As a result, the idea—the dream of an intact, two-parent household—meant more to her than the impact of what we were experiencing. For her, it was stability and survival at any cost.

I know for a fact that it was nothing more than that because as soon as I turned eighteen and moved out, my mother promptly divorced my father and did not look back. She did this even though my brother was still at home because she saw the tension building between them—two men in the house with clashing egos. My brother, a teenager going through puberty with raging hormones, was already bigger than my dad. She worried about conflicts escalating, whether it was over stolen car keys or money. To protect their relationship and prevent potential hostility, she felt it was best for my dad to leave.

It also didn't help that Mom faced severe criticism from her family. She was the so-called black sheep, and their judgments of her and our family were harsh. Some of it came from the belief that my dad was being physically abusive and that she was allowing him to abuse us. The conclusions many drew, however, were mostly from the stereotypes they'd seen on television or conjured in their minds—not from anything they'd ever witnessed. During the years my mom chose to stay, they didn't hold back from openly talking about her.

"She's never going to have anything."

"Her kids ain't going to amount to anything either."

"Monique is going to be one of them fast-tailed girls. Probably going to get pregnant before she graduates high school."

I imagine that these are the voices my mother heard in the back of her mind for years. The painful voices that kept her striving. You'd think that as adults, as her family, they would have seen her struggling to keep her family together and offered assistance of any kind. But nobody wanted to help her. Everybody turned their backs on us. To this day, many of those same family members don't want anything to do with us.

As the oldest, I was criticized the hardest. After hearing about what Aunt So-and-So or Cousin Such-and-Such said, I would always wonder to myself, *Why do y'all hate me so much? Why are you always talking about me? Why am I the villain?*

I've spent years trying to work through the damage their words did to me. How I processed them. I was a very determined, ambitious girl.

What I experienced in my home made me that way. But this also meant that I always felt like I had to prove something to others. I made sure I got good grades and hoped that would impress those family members who used to talk about my mom. I did things I thought would make me good enough. But it never worked. I didn't know then that I shouldn't worry about what anybody has to say about me. I didn't know then that God would have the final say.

Here's a hard pill to swallow: Sometimes your success will happen *in spite of* the people in your life. You won't always have the encouragement and support you need. Even then, trust God. I'm a witness that He will bless you right in front of their faces.

This is especially true on the entrepreneurial journey. There will always be someone out there who will see your light shining bright and make it their mission to dim it. As sad as it is, these family members truly wanted to break my mother. They wanted to break something in me. As a result, they projected their own insecurities and jealousies onto us in very cruel ways. But what their jabs were actually saying was this: *How dare you be great! How dare you be blessed when you come from where you come from! How dare you afford a house when you don't have much money. How dare you exceed my expectations!*

If you happen to be on the other side of this dynamic—the one doing the talking and projecting—I implore you to dig deeper into why you are saying and doing those things. What is it about *you* that's so uncomfortable, so hurt that you need to tear someone down with your words? Don't discount people. Don't count people out just because of what you perceive their home environment or circumstances to be. Don't believe yourself to be better because you have more or know more. Those same family members who called me names went to better schools than me. They had more than we did materially. But where I went to school or how much money was in my mom's bank account—or, yes, even my dad's addiction—did not determine how successful I would ultimately become. Only God could do that.

As I've alluded to, things weren't *all* bad. Every day wasn't dark. One of the good moments I had with my dad was when I was around eleven or twelve, during a time when he was sober. He took me on a train ride on the Metra to downtown Chicago. We went to this little hole-in-the-wall spot for breakfast, and I had steak and eggs for the first time. I didn't even know you could eat steak and eggs for breakfast until that day. It was such a simple thing, but it's one of those memories that remind me of the good times we shared. They help me not to get caught up in the story of his addiction but to remember that many days were filled with love and light and what I now know was the presence of God offering us moments of grace and peace.

Dad tried. As I've mentioned, he went to rehab several times. Each time he emerged clean, we all held on to the belief that he had turned a corner. But each time we watched him fall back into old patterns.

When I was in eighth grade, Dad went to jail for having drug paraphernalia on him. After his short time there, they gave him two years of probation. For the entire two years, he stayed clean. They tested him regularly, and he did not want to go back. During that time, I got to know the real him. All his wonderful traits were on full display. He became very focused on us, his family. He kept a job and worked hard to do right. I learned during those two years that when he had a sober mind, my dad was an amazing, talented man.

Unfortunately, when his probation ended, he returned to using.

Seeing him go back to drugs after that was probably harder than all the years before. Those two years proved that he could do it. With some incentive, he could stay clean. It hurt me so much that his family was not as much of an incentive as jail.

The emotional roller coaster of Dad's addiction was heartbreaking. My mom, my brother, and I stayed on it for what seemed like forever until my sophomore year of high school when my dad was shot four times.

———

Dad is very much a creative—a maker and visionary. Even when he was not well, he was still probably one of the most innovative people I knew. Believe it or not, Dad created Uber before Uber even existed. And that is how he was shot.

Whenever he had a car, Dad would drive around what we called the "low end" and give people rides. Each person would pay him to take them wherever they wanted to go. It was a fairly successful hustle/venture. It got to the point where people would stand outside looking for him.

"Oh, here comes Mickey! He'll give us a ride to the store."

One day, Dad picked up the wrong people. As soon as the young men got in the car, he saw they had guns with them. One man held what appeared to be an AK-47 at his side. Dad was terrified when they hopped in. He just knew they were going to rob somebody. He also knew that if he drove them, he would become an accomplice. But looking at the arsenal of weapons in their hands, what else could he do?

One of the guys told him where to go and, of course, my dad did what the man said. When they arrived at the location, another guy said, "Wait right here! I'm about to go in here and come back. Don't. Move."

Yeah, right.

When the guys got out of the car, Dad hit the pedal hard and sped off. That's when one of the guys started shooting at my dad's car. Four bullets found their way into his back and abdomen as the men ran off and left my dad there to die in the street.

But God said no. Not today.

It just so happened that at that very moment, someone was driving down the street. They saw my dad's body hanging out of the car and called an ambulance. We later learned that this angel was a friend of my great uncle.

Thankfully, the doctors at Cook County Hospital saved my father's life. But there was a consequence to his injuries: He was paralyzed from the waist down, and the doctors didn't hold out much hope that his prognosis would change. Yet, with some physical therapy and God's grace, my father to this day doesn't have to wear a colostomy bag. What's more, with the help of a prosthetic and a bit of a limp, he can walk. God gave him a second chance.

And yet, as soon as Dad got some mobility back, he returned to using. Yes, even after a near-death experience, he couldn't maintain his sobriety. And that completely broke our hearts.

It wasn't until many years later, as I matured and my understanding deepened, that I recognized the full extent of my father's struggles. He still struggles to this day with his sobriety. And I still love him for who he is, not necessarily for who I want him to be. The Bible says to honor our parents, and so I choose to honor him because he's my dad. Although I'm respectful and I continue to pray for him, I also know that he has issues he's dealing with, and this is the only way he knows how to numb whatever unspoken pain he's been through in life. Once I learned to reckon with this, I was able to do my own work of healing. Part of that journey of understanding meant realizing all the lessons I'd learned from the cycle of hope and disappointment that had become a recurring theme in my life.

The first and most profound lesson is the importance of empathy and understanding. It would be easy for me to hate my father for the pain his addiction caused. However, I've chosen to meet him the way Jesus met many people during His three years of ministry on earth. With love. With truth. I've chosen to see the man my dad was when he wasn't under the influence and recognize *that man* as my real dad. Yes, I have unfortunately witnessed his attempts to fight his demons, and yes, it deeply impacted me. But I also know that addiction is a disease, not a choice. Having that lens and a more grace-filled perspective allows me to approach others with more compassion as I recognize that everyone is fighting some battle or another.

I also have empathy because I remember being that little girl living in such uncertainty but still having a dream and holding on to a glimmer of hope that maybe, just maybe, there was something more out there for me. Although I didn't establish a real relationship with God until later in my life, I think I subconsciously understood that He had a purpose for my life beyond the chaos. I chose to believe that. For me, the journey was about figuring out *how* to attain that purpose. I imagine that might be the same for you. How do any of us get from a place where everything in our world is on fire to living our dreams? How do we shut out the noise of others telling us that we're not going to amount to anything?

Very intentionally.

It doesn't matter how you grew up. It doesn't matter whether you were raised amid addiction, abuse, or general chaos—you can still win. You might have some work to do. Some healing to get to. But you can still have a life that's very different from the one you once knew. God may not have put you in that situation, but He did allow for you to endure it and will ultimately work it out for your good, as His Word tells us.

"And we know [with great confidence] that God [who is deeply concerned about us] causes all things to work together [as a plan] for good for those who love God, to those who are called according to His plan and purpose" (Romans 8:28 AMP).

It doesn't matter whether you were raised amid addiction, abuse, or general chaos— you can still win.

Notice this scripture doesn't say all *good* things. It doesn't say all *bad* things either. It's very simple. Continue to love God, to seek His purpose, and anything and everything, past or present, will work together for your good.

I really want you to grab on to that. It's often said that adversity shapes us, and I can attest to that. Because of what I've lived through, I learned some not-so-great things and picked up some patterns that I've had to reconcile. I learned from my mother and her relationship with my father to always keep my guard up no matter what. I learned to trust no one. Fathers are the first loves of their daughters, so when you grow up in an environment where your first love is stealing from you, it is hard to trust. In a household of constant uncertainty, you might not develop the part of you that balances healthy cautiousness with openheartedness. So trusting people—even God to a certain extent—has been a point of healing for me.

But I also know my father's addiction and my mother's resilience forged a path for me. It might seem strange for me to say, but there was absolutely some value in being able to see firsthand what drugs can do to a person, even at a young age. I didn't need a D.A.R.E. program. I didn't need a commercial with a man frying eggs to tell me I shouldn't do drugs. I saw it for myself and steered clear. I knew that drugs could change my appearance and ruin my health because I actually saw it happen. I knew drugs had the potential to tear a family apart because I saw my dad do things he would have never done sober. Even as a teenager, when the people I hung around smoked weed, they all respected my decision to not do it. And it wasn't even because they knew what I was dealing with at home. Nobody knew. Like my mother, I kept everything to myself. I was just strong-willed and gave off the vibe that my boundaries were set. *"Don't even ask Mo because she's not down with that."*

Of course, this is not the model I recommend others to follow. We need support. We need a safe place to lay our burdens down. If you are dealing with something hard, I encourage you to open up to a mentor or friend who can offer encouragement and stability in your life. Asking for support isn't weakness. It's a sign of strength.

And while I was a strong-willed person, I also had a strong mother to lean on. I learned that having one solid person you can trust can take you a long way.

One of the most important lessons I learned from growing up with an addicted

We need support. We need a safe place to lay our burdens down.

parent is the importance of not letting others dictate your future. And more specifically, not letting your circumstances dictate your destiny. No matter how dire my family's situation, there was always this sense that we could rise above it. Especially me and my brother. The narrative that others had about my family was not one I accepted. I refused to be a victim of our circumstances. Instead, I chose to use my experiences as fuel to drive my ambition. I worked hard, excelled academically, and resolved to rise above the stereotypes and prejudices that were projected onto me.

The world may try to impose its limitations on you based on what you look like or where you came from, but it's up to you to break free from those constraints. I am a testament to the fact that no matter how tough your upbringing, you can still achieve your dreams. You can still be great.

The stigma associated with growing up in a household with addiction is a heavy burden, but it was never going to be a life sentence for me. Whatever you might be holding on to doesn't have to be a life sentence for you either. You can overcome the stereotypes and judgments that others place upon you. You can allow God access to the pain of those experiences in order to heal you and transform them into His purpose for your life. The journey may be long and difficult, but the strength and wisdom gained from facing adversity will always serve you well if you let it.

Ultimately, it is not the hardships we face that define us, but how we choose to respond to them. That said, we must be willing to look beyond the specifics of our challenges and focus on the possibilities. We must not lose hope. My father's struggles, my mother's sacrifices, and my own determination have contributed to the person I am today, and I've decided to hold all of my story with gratitude instead of shame. I hope you know that you can do the same.

It is not the hardships we face that define us, but how we choose to respond to them.

QUESTIONS FOR REFLECTION

- Think about a challenging circumstance from your past that has shaped you. How can you reframe that experience to recognize the growth and resilience it has contributed to your life?

- In what ways have you allowed other people's judgments or perceptions to influence your self-image or goals? What steps can you take to release those limitations and embrace the possibilities that God has for you?

Finding Your Person

Guiding Principle:
Choose a partner you can grow with.

I MET MELVIN WHEN I WAS TWELVE. HE WAS IN EIGHTH grade, and I was in seventh. In typical middle-school-girl-of-the-nineties fashion, I saw him on the first day of school and immediately had hearts in my eyes.

"He is soooo cute!" I told my friends.

And he was. Tall and lean, even as an eighth grader, with skin the color of brown sugar, he had a way about him that commanded any room he was in. If he was cracking a joke, everyone was laughing. If he was talking about basketball, everyone was tuned in.

But we didn't hit it off right away. That would take some time.

Over the course of the school year, we got to know each other as we often participated in the same after-school activities. Still, there wasn't any movement toward us having anything more than a friendship. Despite my crush, he was cool, and I was fine with that.

Kind of.

My friends, though, were not having it.

"Girl, you need to find out if he has a girlfriend."

"I'm saying . . . send him a note next time you see him in the hall. Ask him!"

"If you ask, then he'll know you like him without you having to actually say it for real."

I didn't want to send him a note because I was pretty certain he was dating someone, but peer pressure is a thing. I tore out a piece of paper from my notebook and got right to the point: *Do you have a girlfriend?*

I folded the note carefully and—with the kind of artistry only a twelve-year-old girl with a crush could accomplish—gave it to him and waited. The minutes that went by as I watched him unfold the note, look up at me, and then write his answer felt like an eternity. When I got the note back, I was almost afraid to open it. Almost. I finally unfolded the paper and read his response: *Yes, I have a girlfriend.*

Crush. Over.

Having put my toe in the water, I decided that being cordial friends would be all that came from our relationship. I moved on to the next cute boy because . . . seventh grade. Melvin broke up with his girlfriend and started "dating" someone else—this time a girl in my grade. Thankfully, he never said anything about the note. I'm not even sure he really knew how I felt about him. It was mostly the typical middle school back-and-forth and, well, I liked it that way.

Eventually, though, things shifted.

One time he rode his bike to my house when my mom wasn't home. We mostly just talked and laughed about stuff neither of us can remember today. Nothing inappropriate happened. Partly because I was scared of my mom and what she'd do if she found out I had a boy over, and partly because I knew I was way too young to even be contemplating anything more than the junior high, "we go together" shenanigans I was used to. So Melvin rode his bike right back home without so much as a kiss from me. And I'm sure he was very disappointed about that.

We didn't talk for years after that day but that was okay. He graduated from eighth grade and moved on to high school, and, being a year behind him, I remained at our middle school. There were more boys to swoon over and more fun times with my friends. I completely forgot about him.

The next time I saw Melvin was on the school bus. I was now a freshman at the same high school he attended, and there he was again, commanding the attention of everyone on the bus, talking about how he planned to make the varsity basketball team as a sophomore.

Ugh, I thought.

I'm sure I rolled my eyes hard at him too.

Most people are surprised to find out that Melvin and I did not talk or interact the entire remaining three years of high school until he graduated a year ahead of me. What I was once drawn to as a seventh grader—his outspoken, easy, extroverted personality—felt like plain ol' arrogance in my teens. Plus, with everything I had going on at home, I played things close to my chest and was skeptical of anyone who moved differently than I was used to. And Melvin definitely was different. So I went on with my life and he did, too, ultimately graduating and leaving for college.

I wouldn't see Melvin again until the summer before my senior year of high school. He was driving down the street in the nicest car. Guys with cool rides with speaker systems that boomed the latest hit song always attracted girls, and I suppose I was one of them. His red Oldsmobile Cutlass Supreme with chrome rims was everything! And guess what? That seed of affection planted in my adolescence burst out of dormancy. Of course, I tried to ignore my emotions. He was surely the same guy I was not into only a few years earlier, right? At most, we could be friends.

That's what I thought.

During this time, I used my mom's car to get back and forth to work. It was a pain, especially since we never knew when my dad would uncover my mom's keys and take the car out to do what he always did. So after seeing Melvin driving his beautiful ride, I got the bright idea of calling his house—yes, I still had his home phone number from middle school—and asking if he would help me get to and from work. Of course, I wasn't going to tell him that I'd been watching him drive up and down the streets of our neighborhood. It would just be a . . . random call. Actually, he was working for UPS that summer and was rarely home, so I didn't expect him to pick up. (Okay, so maybe I was keeping tabs on him.) When he did, I was stunned.

"Um, hey. What are you doing?" I asked.

I probably should have been more nervous than I was, but I think part of me just wanted to see if he was the same dude who had annoyed me a few years back.

"I'm not doing anything."

And that's really the beginning. We picked up talking like we'd never stopped. Our conversation reminded me of a friend who'd always been around—despite the fact that he had not been around at all.

"I'm going to come over there. I'm going to come to your mom's house."

Here we go.

"Sure, okay."

What else was I going to say? We weren't middle schoolers anymore.

Not too long after we hung up, Melvin came to my mother's house to show off the car I'd already seen a million times. After we talked forever that day, I knew I was in good trouble. He wasn't arrogant at all. Melvin simply had a clear vision of what he wanted from life and wasn't afraid to say it out loud. I liked that.

I don't even remember how we moved from friendship to dating. I think one day he was at my house and said, out of the blue, "Let's go to the show or something." Now, when a guy asks you to go to the movies, it is safe to assume he's asking for a date, so I was excited. Unfortunately, it didn't go as planned.

———

My mom raised me not to wait on any man. That's just what she believed. Her experience with my father taught her that some men could not be depended on, and, inevitably, I took that same stance. On the day we were supposed to go to the movies, I got dressed up and was ready to go. When the pickup time arrived, Melvin was nowhere to be found. He didn't have a cell phone, so there was no way for me to call him and find out what was up. After waiting a while, I picked up my purse and keys and headed to the door.

"I thought Melvin was coming to get you," Mom said.

"Well, he is not here yet, so I'm just going to go ahead and leave," I said.

I can only imagine the proud smirk on my mom's face as I walked out the door. I'm sure she thought, *That's my girl.*

As soon as I left, I called my friends, and we all met up at the movies. Two hours later, I got a call from Mom on my cell.

"Melvin's here. He's looking for you."

I could tell by her voice that she was completely unimpressed with him.

"Well, tell him I'm gone because he didn't come."

And that's exactly what she did. "She left already. I don't know what to tell you."

I'm sure that being this fine, young guy who had girls throwing themselves at him all the time, Melvin assumed I would wait around for him. When I didn't, he probably thought, *Oh, she's not checking for me like that? Wow!* But what's that saying often attributed to Maya Angelou? "You teach people how to treat you." And he learned that day how I expected to be treated.

It wasn't about being mean or petty. I just needed Melvin to know that my time was just as valuable as his. In turn, I think that made him pursue me even more. The next time we set up a movie date, you best believe he was on time. And from there, we spent time together whenever we could between his job working the evening shift and my job and cheerleading camp.

Our summer love was exactly that—a summer love. Not being able to get in touch with him because he didn't have a cell phone and was rarely home started to wear on me. I wasn't willing to fully claim him as my boyfriend if we were going to constantly go days without communicating. That August before my senior year was certainly the seed of something beautiful, but at the rate we were going, that seed was going to die in the ground before it could bloom.

We eventually broke up in the middle of that September—or at least I thought we did. As much as I missed him, I decided it was best that we go our separate ways. But when I started talking to other guys, Melvin started calling me more and more. It was as if, in his mind, we were still together.

"Hey, what's the deal? I hear you're talking to some guy over there. I thought we were still trying to make this work."

I was confused.

"What do you mean? I can never get in touch with you! How are we going to 'make this work' if we don't ever communicate? I don't know *what* we are at this point."

In the back of my mind, I think this was my way of saying, *I'm not going to sit around and wait for you. If you want to pursue me, you're going to have to make more of an effort. I'm not without options.*

As I said, my mother didn't raise me to be thirsty. She was clear about not chasing a guy. She may not have told me verbatim "You're the prize," but that's what she insinuated. *Don't settle. You are the prize.* So I grew up believing that if a guy liked me, if he wanted me, he was going to do what it took to get my attention. And I very much carried that confidence with me when it came to Melvin.

"If you want me, sir, you're going to have to show me."

This has to be one of the greatest pieces of advice my mom gave me, and it's something I want you to carry with you, friend, not just in romantic relationships but in every connection you have. You are worthy of respect, dignity, and having your time valued. If someone doesn't treat you in a way that reflects your worth, it's okay to deny them access to you. In fact, it's necessary.

Part of teaching people how to treat you means knowing you deserve to be treated well. That applies in personal relationships and even in business, which I soon came to learn. When you know your worth, you won't feel pressured to accept just any opportunity that comes your way. It's not about being overly rigid or having impossibly high standards; it's about valuing yourself enough to know that you are enough, exactly as you are.

This is a lesson we should pass down to our children, just like my mom passed down to me. Teaching them self-worth early can change the way they show up in the world. It is the foundation for living with confidence and dignity.

It's not about being overly rigid or having impossibly high standards; it's about valuing yourself enough to know that you are enough, exactly as you are.

After that conversation in September, Melvin and I didn't talk for nearly a month, not even for my birthday in October. When my high school homecoming came around, I was excited and ready to have a good time. I had initially planned to go to the dance with a guy I was seeing at the time, but those plans fell through. In true Monique fashion, I decided to go with three of my friends, and we had such a good time dancing and singing and doing what girls with nothing but hope and dreams and time ahead of them do.

Then, as I was belting out "Hot Boyz" by Missy Elliott, my friend tapped me on the shoulder.

"Guess who's here?" she whispered.

"Who?"

Smirking, she said, "Melvin."

Admittedly, my first thought was, *Um, you are a college freshman. Why are you hanging out at high school homecoming?*

But then I saw him. He was standing by the main door, looking like a lost puppy. When our eyes met, a jolt of joy moved through me. He waved me over and, by the time I reached him, had the biggest smile on his face.

"Guess what?" he said, cool and with his typical swag.

"What?"

"I got a cell phone," he said, showing me the Nokia in his hand and grinning.

"Okay," I said, trying to sound unbothered but really jumping up and down on the inside.

"You want my number?"

Then it was my turn to smile.

"Let's try this again," he continued.

And that was it. That's how he got me back.

Melvin and I were so young when we first started dating. Both of us were dealing with family trauma and all the personal things that go with coming of age. As we were trying to figure out who we wanted to be in this world, some of those growing pains translated into breakups. But there is something amazing about a relationship that's ordained by God. It can withstand growth and change. It can allow room for both people to evolve into all the versions of themselves that are needed to fulfill God's purpose. Our breakups were always brief because, no matter what, our minds and spirits always felt intertwined. Because we connected through traumatic childhood experiences, we both knew how to hold the other's joy and pain in a way no one else could. He came from a home where his mom wasn't involved in his life. I came from a family where my dad struggled to be present because of addiction. We understood what those gaps meant and were able to help each other through the hard parts of navigating them. Regardless of what caused us to break up for two weeks here or a few days there, we were always drawn back to each other.

Melvin saw me. And being truly seen mattered to me in the chaos of my home life. He saw in me qualities that were different from the other girls he knew. He saw in me someone who was a nurturer. Someone he could build a life with. Someone who would take care of his heart. And I saw him too. I saw in Melvin someone who was a protector. His maturity, determination, and potential as a future father attracted me to him.

We weren't like most teenagers. We spent so much of our time together just dreaming. There were times when our dates consisted of driving through wealthy neighborhoods in Chicago and picking out the houses we wanted to live in.

"One day, we're going to have a house like that," we'd say.

"Ooh, look at their garage! I bet you they have a pool too."

We could always envision a better life for ourselves, and that better life always included the other. In fact, I knew I was in love with Melvin when we started discussing our future very early in our relationship. He said over and over again that he saw himself married to me. And I absolutely saw myself as the mother of his children. This ability to see our future so clearly, as well as being able to make amends after a breakup, solidified our feelings for each other.

I know that some women balk at the idea of having to teach a man how to treat them or navigating a series of breakups, but I think it's important to pay attention to who the man is—their history and their true character. Melvin didn't have many good examples of how to treat a woman. I'm not sure he even knew how to date. But he had one thing in his character that made up for it. He was a listener. He paid attention to what I needed and adapted accordingly. That was the green flag. I told him he couldn't be with me if I couldn't communicate with him—and he showed up at my dance like a knight in shining armor, wielding that Nokia phone. He didn't run away. He didn't allow defeat to cause him to give up. He just figured out how to make it work. No talk, just action. I would later learn just how much of a blessing that character trait would be for us, our family, and our legacy.

One of the singular things you will do on your journey to living the life you desire or growing a thriving business is establish partnerships with people who, you hope, are equally invested in your dream. Sometimes that partnership will be romantic. You might have a significant other with whom you plan to do business alongside. Or there might be a best friend who has been with you every step of the way, who has watched you grow into the person God has called you to be. Or maybe you have a business partner who is not a spouse or best friend but is someone who collaborates with you on your entrepreneurial journey. In every case, it's important to be selective about those you allow in your inner circle.

Even Jesus had a kind of "cabinet" among those who followed Him. He certainly loved and did life with all the disciples, but it was Simon Peter, James, and John who, according to Scripture, were His inner circle, the ones for whom He held different expectations (Mark 14:33–34; Luke 9:32–36).

There were levels to His relationships, and He was intentional about who He let in. I've learned to be just as intentional. I invest in self-work and good counsel to ensure that I'm clear about my expectations and that I'm putting people in the right categories. The Bible says, "Do not be misled: 'Bad company corrupts good character'" (1 Corinthians 15:33). Because of this, I'm careful about who I allow into my life. I know the impact they can have on my character and my walk with God. None of Jesus' disciples were perfect, but they all had the character needed to serve in that intimate place in the Messiah's life.

My point is, none of us can build a family or a business on our own. We need people. I encourage you to really think about the following characteristics of good collaborators or partners, and make sure those who are closest to you meet that standard.

When considering a partner (in life or business), be sure that you share the same values. That is the first nonnegotiable in any partnership.

What are your partner's values? I don't think I was mature enough to really understand this with any depth as a teenager, but I did know that Melvin and I believed the same things. Our values aligned when it came to what we wanted in a family and a life. Now that I'm older, it's incredibly important that anyone I closely partner with has a spiritual sense. Do you believe in a power higher than you? Do you believe in God?

None of us can build a family or a business on our own. We need people.

The second thing that's critical in being and having a good partner is recognizing whether each person can support the other without their ego getting in the way. From the very beginning, Melvin showed me his character. He was always a leader, but the *way* he led revealed a person who was team-oriented—even when he was quite capable of getting the job done himself. Whether it's in our home or in Mielle's boardroom, he doesn't allow his ego to get in the way of the goal. He's taught me what it means to be a champion of someone else—to selflessly support another.

When we lost our son, Melvin was the one who kept me emotionally and mentally afloat. Only a few months after our loss, I began writing a business plan for what I thought would be a salon. Whenever things went dark and the waves of grief hit, he'd encourage me to work on my dream. "Go work on your plan," he'd say. Even in the middle of his own heartbreak, he understood just how much this dream distracted me from the more acute pain of grief and helped me heal. He pushed me during that time to not just focus on the loss but shift my attention to something that brought me joy. It's like he knew that this thing I was creating was bringing me happiness in the midst of great despair, and he wanted me to be okay. After the business plan shifted from a salon to hair products and Mielle was launched, Melvin still encouraged me. He never approached the business with ego. I had the vision, yes, but this was *our* thing. And he always kept a "How can I help?" mentality throughout it all.

So whether it is a husband supporting his wife while taking a back seat or vice versa, both people must be able to allow the other person to lead without feeling intimidated. Each person must also understand that both parties' contributions matter. I suppose the real question to pose when choosing a partner is this: Can I be selfless enough to allow my partner to propel the vision, dream, business, or family into destiny?

———

One of the biggest obstacles for new entrepreneurs, especially Black women entrepreneurs, is that we take on a Superwoman complex. I believe it's a generational survival mechanism that has become a generational hindrance. I watched my mom do it. She didn't ask for help. To this day, she doesn't like asking anyone to help her with anything. So many of our mothers, grandmothers, and great-grandmothers were taught that asking for help was a sign of weakness. They felt like they had to do everything themselves because they lived in a world that demanded nothing but labor and isolation from them. However, I have learned—and am teaching my children—that asking for help doesn't make me weak. It's actually a sign of strength. My ability to delegate means I don't have to carry burdens and responsibilities on my own. It means I get to be fully present for my children, my team. I'm able to give the people around me the best version of myself because I'm not pouring out from an empty cup.

Embracing each other's gifts has also expanded Melvin and me in ways we couldn't have imagined. We learn from each other. Yes, Melvin is a logistical mastermind and very business-oriented, but by watching me do my work, he's also become more empathetic. He's grown to understand women's needs since that's our primary audience. In turn, while I am incredibly tuned into our audience and have a great understanding of how to create products that meet their needs and market to them, I've also learned from Melvin how to adopt a firm, more assertive leadership style with the business. This mutual growth has been incredibly instrumental in our personal and business success. Identifying the gifts of those who are on your team and allowing them to operate in that space opens you and your business to remarkable growth.

Once you've found someone who shares your values, the egos are set aside, and you've both learned to allow the other to operate in their gifts, the final way to make a collaboration work is to trust God and the people He sends your way. This is simple, but it's not easy. Nevertheless, trusting God and the people He sends will always work out—if not in your favor, certainly for your good. They will either be a blessing or a lesson. If you haven't met them yet, pray that God sends the right people and gives you the discernment to trust them when they join you on your journey.

> **Trusting God and the people He sends will always work out— if not in your favor, certainly for your good.**

Yes, you *must* trust people.

Trust has been an ever-present theme in my life. Trusting God, trusting myself, trusting other people. So I understand why the idea of trusting might feel hard.

My life has taught me to be very guarded. There are times even now when I still notice my trust issues. But God helps me. Through prayer, I've been able to shift my narrative dramatically from "I trust only You, God, to give me the right people" to "I trust You, God, *and* I'm going to trust these people until they give me a reason not to."

The truth is, if you don't trust the people around you, you will be hard-pressed to accomplish anything. I've found that when I am the most guarded, I also put myself in a position to miss out on the blessings people can be in my life. But since I trust God to be a true coauthor of my life, I also trust and use the discernment He's given me.

God is the ultimate Creator, and He designed perfectly these vessels we walk around in. Our bodies can tell us when something isn't right about a person, but too often we don't listen. Not listening can take us off course. I find that when I do listen, I rarely get it wrong. And if I am still confused about what I'm sensing, I pray. I ask God to reveal what I cannot see.

"What do I do with this information, Father? How do I apply this? Why are You giving me this?"

And guess what? You still might not get it right. That's a hard one, right? How many times have we seen signs that a person is not someone we should partner with but, for whatever reason, we choose to ignore those signs and move forward anyway? We've all done it. Give yourself some grace. You're learning. The best thing to do when you realize you've gotten it wrong is to make the necessary adjustments and move on. It won't be easy, but you can do it. Let the lesson of that experience be the foundation for a future filled with healthy partnerships.

QUESTIONS FOR REFLECTION

- Think about a time when you faced challenges in a relationship or partnership. How did you handle those obstacles, and what did they teach you about setting aside ego and trusting the other person? What qualities do you think are essential for building a strong, collaborative relationship?
- Consider the relationships you're currently investing in. Do these relationships align with your core values and your vision for the future? How might you apply discernment and faith to ensure that you're partnering with someone who encourages your growth and supports your journey?

Surviving the Breakdown

Guiding Principle:
Grief and hope can coexist.

GRIEF IS NOT PREDICTABLE. WE CAN'T SCHEDULE IT OR pack it away into neat little compartments, hoping it will dissolve over time. Instead, grief becomes part of who we are. I'm not sure I truly understood grief until I lost my son. Though I held on to hope and built a strong faith from the experience, I knew deep down that my life—our lives—would never be the same. Not to mention that grief doesn't look the same for everybody. The way I grieved our loss was very different from the way Melvin grieved. And yet we both leaned into that process as much as we could. Sometimes more, sometimes less. The years since our son's passing have taught us that avoiding grief doesn't lessen its weight; if anything, it compounds the pain. Only when we sit with it, acknowledging its presence, can we fully begin to heal.

The day before I went into labor at eight months, I was at home with the girls. It was August 2013, and Melvin had gone to a family gathering. That stands out in my memory because I went to bed alone that night, which was unusual for us. Melvin returned home between eleven o'clock and midnight and quickly fell asleep next to me. About an hour later, a sharp, intense pain in my belly startled me out of my sleep. I grabbed Mel, and when he saw the pain on my face, he immediately jumped into action.

"I'm taking you to the hospital now!" he said as he helped me out of bed.

I was terrified. I'd already had an emergency C-section with our second daughter, so both of us were afraid that I was about to go through the same thing again.

Melvin rushed to wake up the girls, leaving them both in their pajamas and putting them in the car. The next thing I knew, we were speeding off to the hospital.

"Take me to Methodist Hospital, where I had Mackenzie," I said.

My initial thought was to go to Methodist because it was closer. I didn't know how fast these pains would come, and the last thing I wanted was for something terrible to happen while we were still on the way.

"No, I'm taking you where the doctors know you!"

He was right. The doctors didn't know me at Methodist. And I firmly believe that the reason why I ended up needing an emergency C-section with Mackenzie was because of that. The doctor who did my surgery cut my uterus vertically because she claimed that was the only way to get Mackenzie out and save her life. Unfortunately, that vertical incision would create a problem for me in any future pregnancy—including the one with my son.

Once we arrived at the hospital, the nursing staff took me straight to the labor and delivery floor. When they placed me on the monitor, I heard my son's heartbeat and immediately knew it wasn't normal. I'd spent years as a labor and delivery nurse, so I understood the severity of the situation. Unfortunately, the nurses didn't seem to have the same urgency I did.

Nearly incoherent with pain, I cried out, "Where's the doctor? Where's the doctor?!"

As a Black woman, the reality of race-based maternal health disparities is personal and heartbreaking. Too many of us are not heard when we speak up about pain or complications during pregnancy, or we are dismissed by health-care professionals who overlook our voices and concerns because of biases and stereotypes supported by their textbooks. This erasure costs lives—both of mothers and of babies. And these experiences, *our* experiences, are not imagined. There is plenty of data that reveals an alarming trend where Black women are three to four times more likely to die from pregnancy-related complications. We deserve to be heard. We deserve to be treated with respect and given the care that ensures our survival and the survival of our children.

And yet, at that point, there was so much stalling happening. Apparently, the hospital did not have a single on-call doctor available, so they had to call someone in. Meanwhile, the pains kept coming and I could feel my baby was in distress. It felt like I waited an hour for the doctor to finally show up, but it was most likely only about thirty minutes. It didn't matter, though. It was thirty minutes too long when a baby's heart rate is down. When the doctor finally arrived, they rushed me to the operating room and did a C-section—the very thing we were hoping to avoid.

> We deserve to be heard. We deserve to be treated with respect.

My baby boy was born at 1:40 a.m.

"Is my son okay?"

These were my first words after I woke up from the surgery. The look on my mother's face—Melvin had called her while we were on our way to the hospital—told me everything I needed to know. It wasn't good. My heart started beating wildly in my chest.

"Is he pink?" I asked her.

"Yes."

That gave me some comfort. If he was pink, that meant he had gotten at least a little oxygen. I held on to that hope for dear life.

But hours passed. And with every minute that ticked by, I knew things were not going well.

Through all of this, Melvin was absolutely beside himself. He was too distraught to speak. I, on the other hand, was numb. Everything had happened so fast; it was a blur. We were both trying to process what was happening. Finally, the doctor arrived and explained that our son was in the NICU (neonatal intensive care unit), intubated, and his APGAR (appearance, pulse, grimace, activity, and respiration) scores were extremely low. As days went by, more doctors came in to talk to us about his condition and explain his prognosis. Sure enough, the vertical incision from my previous C-section had caused a uterine rupture in this pregnancy, which put me into early labor at thirty-two weeks. Whenever there's this kind of damage, it's highly likely that either the mom passes away or the baby does. Sometimes it's both. It's very, very rare that both make it. The doctor explained to us that because of the rupture, my son had lost a lot of oxygen. Again, the chances of survival were slim. In fact, the doctor said that when he opened me up, he discovered that my baby was already no longer in my uterus. He was in my abdomen.

Those words broke me. I'd seen enough in my career as a nurse to know what they meant. Yet, no matter the numbers or probability, no matter what that voice in the back of my mind was whispering, I chose to hold on to hope. I needed a miracle.

At the same time, I was also dealing with my own physical recovery from the labor and surgery. I had lost a lot of blood and needed a transfusion. In my pain-filled fog, I listened as the doctor told me that he was able to save my uterus, despite my having the rupture. When there's a uterine rupture, a hysterectomy is generally necessary. However, the risk in performing the hysterectomy is bleeding out. The doctor was able to at least prevent that. But again, I still lost blood and still required both a transfusion and a week-long recovery in the hospital, on top of the typical recovery after a C-section. None of that mattered to me, though. I would endure whatever was necessary if it meant that my baby and I got to eventually leave the hospital together and whole.

We were so grateful for the pastors, family, and friends who supported us in those immediate days after I gave birth. So many of them came to the hospital and sat with our baby in the NICU as I was recovering and Melvin was tending to our girls. We prayed over my son constantly, hoping he'd wake up. We vigilantly watched all the machines that were connected to his precious body—especially the EEG attached to his head that monitored seizure activity. Nearly every day, he would have a seizure, and every time it happened we prayed and cried, and prayed and cried some more. It felt like torture. But I still held on to the belief that his story would be different.

Lord, please let him come out of this.

I needed some of those prayers for myself too. About a week after I gave birth, while we were visiting our son in the NICU, I began to feel very nauseous. Then I started vomiting profusely, to the extent that the medical team rushed me to the ER for immediate care. It was there I learned that I had a bowel obstruction. It seems that the doctor who performed my C-section and "saved my uterus" also nicked my bowels while inside. That explained why anything I tried to eat came right back up. After the trauma of an emergency C-section, I was now back in the hospital for another week with an NG (nasogastric) tube stuck up my nose and down my throat to help heal the bowel obstruction.

I felt like I was losing my mind.

In light of his needs, my son was eventually transported to a more advanced NICU at the University of Chicago Medical Center. Unfortunately, over the next few months, the prognosis didn't improve. We were told multiple times that he wasn't going to make it. But again, that was utterly inconceivable to us. We weren't ready to give up. Every day we prayed, read scriptures, and sought hope wherever we could find it. We had pastors pray over him at his bedside, and we clung to the hope that God would change our baby's course.

After four months of that, Melvin and I became frustrated with the University of Chicago because it felt like they were trying to force our hand to take our son off life support. They had given up, and that hurt. In hindsight, I realize that we were in denial about what was possible for our baby boy. We were desperate and hoping for a different outcome. We were still praying for a miracle. Around the five-month mark, we made the difficult decision to transfer our son to Northwestern Memorial Hospital, still holding on to the slim chance that something might change. And once again, the doctors at Northwestern were not hopeful. Our boy had been on life support for six months, growing physically but with no brain function. His body was here, but he did not have any consciousness.

I think deep down, I knew. I knew my son wasn't coming home. But I couldn't say that out loud. There was a finality to speaking those words that I wasn't willing to embrace. But as the days and weeks and months stretched on, it became harder and harder to hold on to hope. It was clear that my son was suffering. Every day the doctors urged us to take him off life support, and every day we refused. Melvin and I leaned on each other in a way we'd never done before even as grief inched its way into our minds and hearts. And of course, we were still trying to be present for and take care of our daughters.

———

Like many who endure tragedies that turn their world upside down, Melvin and I turned to the church for solace. Before this, we had a knowledge of, even a belief in, God. As I've shared, there were certainly times I prayed, especially as a teenager. But neither of us went to church regularly, and religion felt very abstract in our lives. There was a vast distance between our general understanding of there being a creator of the universe and the intimate relationship with a Savior that I believe our souls were longing for—especially at this moment in our lives.

Then, on a Sunday when I thought my grief was going to undo me, I met Jesus.

That day, I took step after ordered step with Melvin toward the altar call of a church we'd been casually attending. I felt so lost. It was like I was in the middle of a complete breakdown on the inside as I tried to understand why my baby boy was being taken from me. That's when a woman with soft eyes and a fiery tongue laid her hands on us and began to pray. To this day, I call her our angel because, given the size of the church and the fact that the altar was crowded with people, it could not have been anyone but God guiding her to us. That prayer spoke to everything I was going through at that moment. It was like she knew everything—as if God sent her specifically to tell me that we would survive this heartache. After she prayed, Melvin and I looked at each other and silently agreed: *This is our place. This is our church.* There was just something about that community of believers. It was clear that God was real and He was there.

There is no doubt in my mind that through this woman I'd never seen before, God was telling me that He was with me. He was with us. He was telling us that He was intimately acquainted with our grief and would walk us through it, no matter the outcome. By giving our lives to Christ that day, we were ensuring that we would have the strength to emerge from this pain better. But there was definitely going to be more pain. Because it was time to let go.

Melvin and I finally came to peace with the decision to take our son off life support. Yes, the doctors had been saying this. But it needed to be a decision we made with God's guidance and not because of a doctor's report. Despite how much pain we experienced throughout the process, I'm still proud that we did it on our terms. That we didn't allow the hospital to force us to let go before we were ready—before we heard God tell us to release him. We wanted our sweet Milan—that is his name—to know that we had done everything we could to keep him here with us. We wanted him to feel our love—a love that transcended his consciousness. We took him off life support the second week of January 2014, and he passed away about an hour later.

Even though his time here was short, Milan's life had a purpose. I believe that. He was on an assignment from God because I know I would not have come to know God the way I do now if it hadn't been for his life and death. To be clear: God didn't cause his death. God wasn't torturing us to get us to come to Him. A loving God wouldn't do that. He doesn't have to do that. But an all-knowing God can see the outcome of our physical frailties as humans well before we can. So in light of the very real trials of life and living, God often sets things up for our good in the aftermath of it all. He allows the results of our humanity to have a positive impact.

God often sets things up for our good in the aftermath of it all.

That said, I believe that God chose me in a way. In order for me to do the work I do now, to serve people in the ways I do now, I had to go through this hard thing so I could really see and know His transformative power. It's complicated, for sure, but I know if I had not lost my son, I would likely be trying to do this life on my own. Now I know I don't have to. I don't have to have it all figured out. Going through this kind of loss can break you. It almost broke me. But when I learned there was a God I could lean on, it gave me the strength to keep going. Every morning that I read the Bible and listened to praise and worship music before heading to the NICU, God was refilling my cup. He was giving me beauty for my ashes (Isaiah 61:3).

Milan's assignment wasn't just for me, though; it was for my entire family. My husband, our oldest daughter, and I all found faith through this experience, and now we share our testimony with others, bringing more people to God's kingdom. Mielle has over two hundred employees, all who have been inspired by the Melvin and Monique Rodriguez testimony. Would that be true if Milan didn't complete his assignment? I really don't think so. And in that way, Milan's six-month journey on earth was absolutely an embodiment of the gospel.

In the aftermath of our son's passing, Melvin and I leaned on each other more than ever. He was my rock, always encouraging me, even when I didn't have the strength to get out of bed. He kept me busy, motivated me to start dreaming again, and made sure we spent time as a family in order to create a kind of new normal for us and our daughters. We also had the support of our church community, who surrounded us with love and care.

———

It's been more than ten years and there's one thing I know for sure: Grief doesn't just disappear. There is no expiration date. It comes in waves, sometimes when we least expect it. It comes on the edges of memory and imagination. There are days when I think about how Milan would be in fifth grade now. Possibly loving his video games or getting a kick out of teasing his older sisters. That dream causes the tears to flood my eyes and makes my heart swell with sadness. But resisting that grief only makes the pain stronger. Instead, I let it wash over me. I allow myself to cry, to remember, to feel the depth of my pain. And in doing so, I also allow myself to heal a little more each time.

Over the years, I've learned to hold the joy in those moments too. The joy being that, with every new rendering of what might have been, I am keeping Milan's memory alive. There's no right or wrong way to grieve. Everybody grieves differently. Allowing myself the space to remember who he was and who he might have been is my way of letting my grief be heard. Some people may go to the gravesite of their loved one and put flowers on a headstone. Others may choose the person's birthday as a day to celebrate them—something we used to do before it became too difficult. Although these aren't things I can do because it's still too painful, I do have his photo as my screensaver on my phone. Melvin asked me once, "Why do you keep him on your screensaver?" And I said, "Because that's my way of always keeping him with me in my heart." I have found ways to honor his memory without dwelling in the pain.

There's no right or wrong way to grieve. Everybody grieves differently.

And of course, Mielle Organics wouldn't exist if it weren't for him. As much as *Mi-elle* means "my girls," that "Mi" also holds the memory and presence of Milan. Every major project we work on is named after him or his birthday. He's always with us, and his legacy continues through the work we do.

———

Please know that grieving and hoping are not mutually exclusive. During those tenuous months while Milan was in the NICU, I simultaneously grieved the loss of my son while still holding on to hope for a miracle. I know that seems like a contradiction, but I lived it. I saw the numbers. I knew the odds. But what kept me hopeful was when I'd go to his bedside and read the Bible to him. I would read scriptures or pray, and there was this sense that he could hear me. He could hear his mommy reading to him or praying for him, and it was helping him in some way—even if it just gave him peace. Of course, there were also days when I didn't know what to pray for. When I didn't know how to ask for his healing. And in those moments, I would just sit still and let the tears flow.

I should clarify that grief isn't always about the loss of a loved one, as I experienced. It shows up in many ways. Grief might rear its head at the end of a relationship, the loss of a job, or the failure of something you poured your heart into. I've felt this personally, grieving friendships I thought were solid, only to realize they weren't what I believed. Letting go of those relationships meant mourning the loss of something I once valued deeply.

Even my mom experienced grief in an unexpected way. After dedicating forty years of her life to her job at the University of Chicago, she faced the harsh reality of a pension and retirement package that fell short of her expectations. She had to grieve the fact that all her hard work didn't amount to what she believed it would. It's these kinds of losses—the ones that reshape our expectations and force us to confront painful realities—that people often overlook as real grief.

To anyone grieving something deemed "smaller," I want you to know it's okay to feel how you feel. Grief is a process, and there's no right or wrong way to go through it. But it's essential to move toward acceptance and not stay stuck in despair. Surround yourself with people who genuinely care and want to help you heal, and lean into God's Word for encouragement. Remember, your emotions are valid, but they don't define your path. Grief can teach you, but it doesn't have to keep you.

Whatever grief looks like for you, know this: You're not going to be able to escape holding the tension of grief and hope, even many years after your loss. Really, for the rest of your life. But that's not a bad thing. If anything, it's a strength. Don't see the embracing of grief as meaning you have to wallow in your sorrow. No! What it means is that you have a superpower. It means you give yourself permission to feel everything—both the pain and the joy—in any given circumstance. Grief doesn't diminish us. In fact, it is God's magnificent way of giving us great compassion, for ourselves and others.

Your emotions are valid, but they don't define your path.

QUESTIONS FOR REFLECTION

- How has grief shaped your view of hope and healing? In what ways can you allow yourself to feel both the sorrow and the joy in your journey without one diminishing the other?
- Consider the ways you honor the memories of loved ones you've lost. How can these practices provide both comfort and a sense of connection?

Embracing God's Plan in the Pivot

Guiding Principle:
Check who or what is driving your decisions.

IN BUSINESS, WE OFTEN HEAR ABOUT SELF-RELIANCE.
We read books about having grit and putting in the work. We live in a culture where being self-made is celebrated. But my experience has taught me that self-reliance has its limits. There was a time early in my career when I thought I had it all figured out.

Remember that salon I was going to open? At the time, I believed success was something I could achieve only through hard work, ambition, and my own strength. Like many, I made plans and set goals, thinking that if I just pushed hard enough, I would get there. But what I came to realize is, my plans, while well-intentioned, were limited. I couldn't see what those who mentored me could see. I didn't know what they knew. Thankfully, my heart was open enough to listen. I considered their words to be a nudge from God, telling me to pivot. Instead of stubbornly sticking to my original plan, I received their feedback as confirmation from God that I was meant to do something different. From there, Mielle was born.

Pivoting isn't easy, and there's not always a straightforward way to recognize when God is calling you to change directions versus when it's your own fear or hesitation causing you to be distracted. Nevertheless, God will let you know. And sometimes He will use people as vessels to deliver those messages. For me, I often get a gut feeling about something early on. Then, seemingly randomly, God will send someone into my life to confirm it. In fact, I think most of the time whenever we receive God's word through other people or external sources, it's usually a confirmation of things we have already felt in our bodies but were afraid to acknowledge. I don't believe in coincidences. When I felt unsure about starting a business, God sent people to remind me of my calling. When I was contemplating a partnership, God sent people to affirm what I already sensed. And even now, with the success I've had, whenever I am tempted to give up or go back to my comfort zone, God keeps pulling me toward something greater.

We can make all the plans we want, but those plans can only take us so far. Trusting in God's greater plan, however, takes us further than we could ever imagine. When I trust His direction in my life and business, it affords me the capacity to pivot, adapt, or release when necessary. This way, I know that when I pray and seek God's guidance, I'm positioning both myself and my business for success.

Please understand, it's 100 percent okay to make your plans. It's critical to do so. You'll need a business plan to launch your dream. You'll need a marketing plan to promote that dream. You'll need a written vision of where you'd like that dream to go. I've made plenty of plans on this journey, and I'm a firm believer that we need to have a sense of direction and goals to strive toward. However, while it's good to have a plan, it's critical that we're willing to be malleable and leave room for God to establish that plan. We must always be listening for God to provide us the route to execute our plans. Proverbs 16:9 says, "In their hearts humans plan their course, but the LORD establishes their steps." My plans may be good, but God's plans are always greater. Like a GPS, through prayer I might set my destination, the place I'd like to go. But I need to allow the voice of God to provide the directions on how to get there safely and with minimal obstacles. He can see the road better than I can, that's for sure.

Most would call this adaptability. In business—in all of life—it's important not to get stuck in one way of thinking. That kind of rigidity will only limit your growth. As entrepreneurs, we need to be like chameleons, able to adapt to the changing seasons while staying true to who we are.

Is this something you tend to embrace or resist? I encourage you to lean into necessary change to adapt in our world and to have the foresight to see where your business or industry is going so you can figure out how to adjust. That way you're not left behind or pigeonholed into a specific category. It's very easy in this business climate, and perhaps life in general, to find yourself boxed in because you weren't willing to change.

———

One of the greatest examples of my being obedient—of listening closely to God's voice and pivoting my plan accordingly—came at the very beginning of my journey as an entrepreneur. After experiencing the loss of my son, I was in a place of deep grief. But God spoke to me in that season, giving me His vision for Mielle, and I felt a strong sense of purpose attached to what I was supposed to do with this company. Yes, we were making hair products. And yes, we wanted to be successful at making hair products. But it wasn't about *just* making money or becoming traditionally successful. According to what God was showing me, those things would simply be by-products of something greater. His plan was for me to use my gifts and my story to bless others.

Starting Mielle was a complete act of faith. Melvin was working at UPS, and I was still working as a nurse, this time in home health care. We had two children and not a lot of disposable income. How in the world were we going to buy the materials we needed to make and package products and then have the time to sell those products to consumers and salons? I had absolutely no idea. I couldn't see how it would all unfold, but I had confidence in God's promise. So we sacrificed where we could. Melvin focused on the business during the day and worked at UPS in the evenings. I worked the business in the evenings after the kids went to sleep. I prayed, journaled, and decided to invest time in understanding how to do this thing called social media that had just taken off over the last few years. The rest was in God's hands.

And honestly, that's the essence of making God-inspired decisions. It's not about having all the answers up front; it's about doing what you can and then surrendering the rest to God. It's about trusting that God's plan will lead you exactly where you need to be, even if the path looks uncertain.

I haven't always been so willing to surrender, though. When I look back at times when I didn't trust God's guidance, when I tried to control every outcome, I can see how much energy I wasted. For example, when I was still working as a nurse and tried *twice* to go back to school to pursue a master's degree in nursing, life got in the way both times. I now know that God was trying to pull me toward entrepreneurship. That's the reason I dabbled in various multilevel marketing opportunities and other side hustles at the time. I resisted the big vision at first. I kept doubting myself. I didn't think I was capable of running the kind of business I saw in the vision He gave me. It felt too far-fetched to see myself at the helm of a global beauty brand. So for a while, I stayed in my comfort zone because that's what I knew.

Breaking out of that thinking and starting Mielle anyway was a major pivot—first, from self-reliance to God-reliance. And let me tell you, it wasn't comfortable. I went from a place of certainty, where I knew my role as a nurse, to uncharted territory, where I had to trust God to guide me in a business I didn't know very well. But once I surrendered my plan to God, everything began to fall into place. I started Mielle Organics, and the business took off in ways I never could have imagined. I now know that even when I make mistakes or take a wrong turn or wait too long to pivot, God will bring me back to where I need to be, as long as I stay in relationship with Him.

Even since starting the company, there have been times when I've leaned too much on my own understanding instead of letting God direct my path (Proverbs 3:5–6). In every instance, though, God has quickly and concisely let me know when and where I've gotten off track, and I've course corrected immediately. I've seen too many times how God's direction has led to my elevation, so I'm never going to stray too far off His path for me.

———

One of my most compelling arguments for why trusting God's guidance will lead to bigger and better places is the story of how Mielle became a household name in the first place. I've always believed in staying ahead of the curve. When new technology or new ideas emerge, I don't hesitate. I become determined to learn what I need to learn and find the right people with the expertise to help adopt the practice. When Instagram first became popular, many of the established brands didn't know what to do with it. The world was moving fast, and technology was evolving even faster. Companies weren't sure if posts and likes would translate into sales and brand recognition. So after some prayer, I envisioned an opportunity. I knew we didn't have time to sit back and watch how other brands approached social media. Instead, I figured out how to make it work for us immediately.

Having listened closely to God's direction in other areas of my life, I'd already learned to be quick to pivot, so this shift felt easy. Mielle was a tiny, young, hungry company that was willing to learn. So while my competitors were hemming and hawing, trying to figure social media out, I dove in headfirst, posting videos on how to use our products and creating an intimate community of followers who became brand ambassadors in their part of the world. As a result, Mielle Organics quickly became a leading brand on the major social media platforms. While big brands were still playing it safe, we took a chance and ultimately—by executing an innovative marketing strategy—disrupted the industry, for no other reason than we weren't afraid to try something new, even if it meant taking risks.

And that's another thing—faith often requires you to take calculated risks. But calculated doesn't always mean that people will understand it. Sometimes taking risks means looking a little foolish—and that's okay. You might try something and fail, but at least you tried. You learned what worked and what didn't.

Faith often requires you to take calculated risks.

But what if you don't fail? What if you win? Stay curious. Be willing to discover something new and exciting. Let the newness of the pivot energize you. You may not know how it will all work out, but if you trust God's plan, you can move forward with confidence.

Here's the catch to this trusting God thing: You can't be obedient to someone you don't know. If you don't have a relationship with God, how will you know when He's telling you to pivot or adapt? I believe that was what was different from all the other businesses Melvin and I tried before. With Mielle, we'd begun our walk with Jesus. There was a real desire to recognize His voice and allow Him to lead us into this new space. My ability to pivot and adapt has been one of the greatest gifts in my business journey, but it all stems from trusting God's direction first.

If you look at the world today, it's changing so fast. What was once considered the norm in any area of business has shifted dramatically. Because of this, I know that if I don't adapt, my business will get left behind. I've always been able to make small adjustments and see positive results from those changes. But the goal is to scale my ability to pivot in the same ways that I would scale a business. So yes, I do recommend that you start with small adjustments. Practice with low-stakes changes. But ultimately, work up to being able to make the big, life-changing pivots if necessary.

I encourage you to be observant—study people, stories, and those who possess what's called "adaptability IQ." It's the measure of how quickly we can adapt to changing circumstances. In my observation, those who are less able to adapt to change—whether in business or in their personal lives—struggle. If that's you, it doesn't mean that God can't or won't grace you. Or that struggling with change means you're lost completely. I don't believe that. But I do believe that you will gain an advantage when you can hear God's direction clearly and then shift gears accordingly, without hesitation.

So what does it take to have a high adaptability IQ? First and foremost, it's your attitude and perspective. Try to approach unfamiliar situations with a good attitude and integrity. Instead of dreading a challenge, ask yourself, *What can I learn from this?* Even the Bible tells us to work with integrity because we're working for the Lord, not for man (Colossians 3:23). When you have a positive attitude, people around you won't even realize you might not be completely at ease with your current situation.

For example, when I worked as a nurse, I didn't always like the minutiae of my job. But my patients and coworkers never knew that. I always showed up with a smile because I didn't want anyone to say, "Monique has a bad attitude." While I don't care what people say about me, I do care how I make them feel. I believe it's essential that no one ever feels inadequate or less than when they interact with me, because I represent God's kingdom. Everyone deserves to feel like a decent human being.

I believe your attitude is also related to how God trusts you with bigger responsibilities. If you show up with a positive attitude, God knows He can trust you with more. When He eventually gave me two hundred employees at Mielle, He knew I would treat them with the same kindness and consideration I showed as an employee myself. And yes, it's hard not to complain when you're in a bad job. I get that. But realize that being negative is not the answer. God could very well be preparing you for what you ultimately want.

———

Another key to adaptability is having a growth mindset, not a fixed one. I know that phrasing is somewhat cliché nowadays in the business world, but it doesn't make it any less true. People with a fixed mindset are stuck in the present moment. They can't see beyond their current circumstances. They aren't hopeful, and they often attract negativity. They don't realize that situations are temporary and can change.

Another key to adaptability is having a growth mindset, not a fixed one.

On the other hand, a growth mindset helps you see opportunities for learning and development in every situation. Nothing you go through is in vain. Every experience is shaping you into the person God has created you to be.

When you have a growth mindset, you also understand that you don't have to be a victim. Even when you've been victimized, you can choose how you will respond. Instead of dwelling on what happened, you can look at your situation and ask, *How can I learn and grow from this?* Then, once you heal, grow, or change, you are able to reach back and help others avoid the same mistakes.

Please be mindful that having a high adaptability IQ does not equate to knowing it all and having everything figured out before making a move. Too many people don't even start moving forward because they feel like they don't have enough information. But that's a strategy of the Enemy, who wants you to stall and never achieve your dream. When I'm embarking on something new, I learn what I can. But I don't let what I don't know stop me from taking the step God has told me to take. I don't have to completely understand the path ahead. I just need to take the first step in the direction of God's voice. He is the One making the way. All I have to do is trust Him and submit to His will.

Of course, fear is real. It's scary out there. In the world of business, many of us are leaping into what seems like pure darkness. I've faced internet trolls, industry competitors, and people who just didn't believe in my vision. I'll talk more about this in a future chapter, but know this: Every time I face criticism or negativity, I remember that my work is for God, not for man. I encourage you to remember that. It's what I'm telling my children when I repeat to them something I heard T. D. Jakes say in a sermon years ago, which in effect was, "giraffes don't entertain or engage with turtles."[1] That's how you must view those who exist in the darkness. They are not on your level, so don't waste time conversing with them or worrying about their opinions.

This is where resilience is important. You cannot avoid people who will try to knock you down. There will always be those who are going to tell you no. In my experience, this often happens when you're successful and growing very fast. But I know that what God has ordained and anointed, no man can touch. I'm protected.

Still, having tough skin is vital. As you embrace upcoming pivots or changes, ask yourself, *Am I strong enough to face being knocked down? What is my plan for picking myself up?* And if nobody's there to motivate or encourage you, then you'll need to motivate and encourage yourself.

Even in the face of industry competition, I've often had to focus on my work and let it speak for itself. This is especially true as I've dealt with unhealthy forms of competition over the years. In every case, my instinct has been to defend myself loudly. Or to immediately confront the problems head-on. In some instances, that's necessary. But often, I've had to learn that what my competitors say and think about me is none of my concern.

Navigating these kinds of trials in business can be incredibly painful. You might even find yourself saying, "Are You sure, God?" It's easy to wonder if the path God is leading you down is worth all the trouble and negativity. But I know that trusting God will always be the right move. And at the end of the day, the actions of others are not a reflection of me. Honestly, it's not even a matter of me saying, "Ooh, those competitors or influencers are just so jealous of me." It's deeper than that. Too many of those same entrepreneurs are acting out of a mindset of scarcity. They believe that there can only be one success in the field. This is especially true for a Black woman.

For so long, the system has been structured to allow for only one or two Black-owned businesses to crack that glass ceiling and scale their business globally. Despite this slowly changing, many of those same people will unfortunately always struggle with those of us who choose to operate from a mindset of abundance. They can't fathom the belief that there's enough room for all of us to win. But I believe it because I know God's plan for me. I trust it. And I know that no one can steal it, no matter how hard they try. Romans 8:31 says, "If God is for us, who can be against us?" I don't worry about competition because I know, no matter the opposition, if I'm following God's path, no one can stand in the way of His plans for my life and my business.

When I think about how far I've come, I'm grateful for every challenge, every setback, and every pivot. They weren't comfortable, but they were necessary. They taught me to trust God in every aspect of my life and business. I appreciate the saying by Dr. Martin Luther King Jr.: "Faith is taking the first step even when you don't see the whole staircase."[2]

I encourage you to check who's driving your decisions. Seriously! Let go of the need to control every outcome and trust God's direction. Lean into the pivot and embrace the big changes that will inevitably come. God sees the bigger picture, and His plans are far greater than anything you could imagine. Again, go ahead and make your plans. Set your goals. But always leave room for God to guide you. When you do that, you'll find yourself on a path that not only leads to success

God will take you further than you could ever go on your own.

but to a deeper understanding of who you are and what you're called to do. God will take you further than you could ever go on your own.

QUESTIONS FOR REFLECTION

- Think about a time when you felt called to pivot or change direction in your life or career. What inner signals or external guidance helped you recognize this need for change, and how did you respond?
- Reflect on your current decision-making process. Do you find yourself relying solely on your own understanding, or do you leave room for divine guidance? How can you incorporate intentional faith-based discernment into your daily choices?

One Step Forward

Guiding Principle:
Just start.

STARTING MIELLE ORGANICS WAS NEVER ABOUT JUST creating hair care products. If I'm honest, in some ways it was about filling a void. Finding a purpose that was long-lasting. Something that made my grief meaningful. It was also a way to connect with my community. In fact, that was probably the biggest motivation of all. Mielle was born from both passion—my love for all things beauty—and pain. Both of those things, and the healing that came as a result, shaped its foundation.

In the beginning, I was simply sharing my hair care journey on social media. I had always been fascinated by how different ingredients affected the health and texture of my hair, so I started experimenting—mixing oils with conditioners, playing with all kinds of ingredients I found right in my kitchen. I used food products like honey and eggs to create concoctions and then shared with my Instagram followers. But I quickly realized that while the results were amazing, none of the products were stable enough to be sold. The eggs and mayonnaise would surely spoil if

I tried to ship them, and that wasn't the experience I wanted for people who tried anything with my name on it.

But as I continued to play in my hair, a vision became clear: I wasn't just giving my internet friends tips. I was empowering and educating women about how to have healthy hair. I was sharing with them ways to take care of their hair without putting fifty-eleven chemicals in it. And these women were excited! I realized this was exactly the feeling I wanted people to have if I were to create my own brand of hair products. Because that's what having a brand is about. It's about how people feel when they see your brand logo. The feedback I received told me that the way people felt when they saw or used my product mattered just as much as the results. That was my light bulb moment!

I needed to figure out a way to bring these ideas to fruition and validate them. And the only way I was going to do that was to find an expert in the field. Being a nurse and having taken courses like organic chemistry, I knew how to mix a few things, but I was not a chemist. I had a rudimentary understanding of most of it, but I could not put formulas together. That required my taking on a manufacturing partner who could help with that. I needed someone with the technical expertise to take my kitchen recipes and make them into something stable and effective.

When we step into anything new, there's a moment when we have to accept whatever learning curve lies before us and be willing to not only educate ourselves but also build a team that will support what we're trying to do. For me, it was about understanding that I didn't have to know everything or have all the answers right away. At the beginning I brought on a chemist and later utilized the logistical expertise of my own husband to execute what I saw in my head. I was equipped with everything I needed for the journey—including the people who would help me along the way. And I had to trust that. Even when beta tests didn't work. Even when mistakes were made. The entrepreneurial journey was teaching me that God never calls us to something without giving us the resources to succeed. Even if we can't see how it will all come together, He already has the blueprint. All we need to do is take the first step, and then one step at a time moving forward.

Once I realized I needed a chemist to help make my product shelf-stable, I began the search for a company that could help bring my vision to life. Call after call after call was made to any and every entity in the Midwest. I had a clear idea of what I wanted the products to do for my customers' hair, but I needed a partner who could turn those ideas into something that could be sold and used long-term. I wanted to hold that bottle in my hand! But as I continued reaching out to manufacturers, I kept hitting roadblocks. Most of them had very high minimum-order requirements—ten thousand units or more—and being a small, home-based business at the time, I simply couldn't afford that.

There will always be obstacles when starting a business, beginning a new job, or changing careers—or really, when starting any new season in life. People will tell you no, doors will close, worry or anxiety might set in, and there will certainly be times when you wonder if you are even on the right path.

What dreams do you have in your heart right now that are on the brink of dying? I encourage you to treat every no as a "not yet" or a "no, I have something better." In other words, each no is just a step closer to the yes that God has waiting for you. Even as I struggled to find a chemist or manufacturer, I had to remind myself that God wouldn't have placed this vision in my heart if there wasn't a way for it to come to pass.

After countless rejections and in my last hour of making calls, I finally found a local manufacturer right there on the South Side of Chicago. I reached out to them and my very first question was, "What's your minimum?" I didn't want to waste any more of my time. When they told me they required a small minimum order, my heart leaped with joy. This felt like a breakthrough. "Oh, perfect. Can I come meet with you all?"

Each no is just a step closer to the yes that God has waiting for you.

They agreed, and I immediately got in my car and drove to their facility. After the meeting, we made sure that the facility was FDA approved, signed an agreement, and began the process of testing and tweaking until we got everything just right. Once the formulas were finalized, we moved on to the next steps: packaging, labeling, and getting the product ready for sale. Mielle was on its way.

But even before we had a finished product, I was working on building anticipation. The community I'd created on social media was anxious to see where all my experimentation had led me. Simultaneously, I started looking for different in-person events to attend. Now, as a natural introvert, this was incredibly hard. It required me to step outside of my comfort zone. Thankfully, my work as a nurse had helped me. Engaging with patients and their families facing varying states of illness and distress, as well as learning to adjust and adapt constantly to whatever was happening in the room, was incredibly helpful for this new phase of my life. So if there was a networking or empowerment event happening in Chicago, listen, Monique was there. I wanted to get in front of women and do what I called "seeding the market." In a way, that was also a complete act of faith. I was out there talking about my brand and discussing products that had not even come out yet. Planting seeds that I hoped would grow and flourish. If you want to dream big, you've got to act big too.

If you want to dream big, you've got to act big too.

I gave out teasers and directed people to our social media pages, where I would upload pictures of the various events. I began letting my followers in on the process, sharing updates whenever I received samples from the manufacturer. Doing that created excitement around the brand before we even launched. These were my people. They would ultimately become the ambassadors for the brand because they had been watching me grow all along and were invested in seeing me take these small steps toward something bigger.

Ironically, though, the first official event where we had an actual product to sell was rather small. We had a table display at a mom-and-pop beauty supply shop in the Bronzeville area of Chicago. The owners sold other products, but this gave us an opportunity to be discovered by future customers.

I know in the beginning people were watching me and saying, "Why is this girl putting egg and mayo in her hair and posting about it on social media?" I even got phone calls from friends who were like, "What in the world are you doing?" Some were asking out of curiosity. Others were asking to be a Negative Nancy. But I didn't pay either group any mind.

They were watching me. And eventually, they would catch on.

"Oh, you are about to start a hair line?"

Exactly.

Whether people are supporting you from the jump or cautiously lurking to see if you can actually accomplish what you set out to do, they are all fans. I welcomed them all because those watching eyes translated into engagement, and engagement meant the algorithm would work in my favor when the product dropped.

We had a good turnout for that first event—more than we expected. I'm sure many people showed up because they were nosy, but again, those bodies in the building mattered when it came to building momentum. Even if they weren't going to buy something immediately, they were certainly going to talk about Mielle. And early in the entrepreneurial journey, word of mouth matters more than anything.

As sales continued, that word of mouth grew. There is no amount of marketing that could replace the power of a great product and genuine connections with customers. And isn't that the way God works? When we pour love and care into what we create, others can feel it, and they want to be part of it. It's as though God amplifies what's done in faith and multiplies the impact beyond what we could ever imagine.

After launching three more products, the verdict was finally in: Our audience loved it. Women were saying their hair felt so soft after using it. Some were even calling our conditioner the new "Creamy Crack" because it softened the hair so much, it was almost as effective as getting a full relaxer.

I knew that once people saw us getting great reviews, even the doubters would not be able to resist trying us out. And once they did, they were going to be hooked. That's the ripple effect our initial launch caused.

Since then, watching this community—Mielle's community—grow has been one of the most rewarding parts of my journey. Focusing on building relationships with my Mavens and Mavericks, sharing their reviews and feedback about the product on social media, and showing them that their voices mattered paid off for us early on and continues to pay off to this day. I didn't want to just sell my people a product—I wanted to create a movement. And that's what Mielle became: a movement of women empowered by the knowledge that they could achieve the results they wanted.

———

The fact that God often asks us to walk by faith and not by sight—especially as believers in the business world—is no joke. The launch of Mielle was fantastic, but there were also so many moments when I couldn't see how things were going to work out. Still, I kept believing.

When we finally launched Mielle Organics, we were overwhelmed by the response. We started with just one product, the hair oil, and one hundred bottles of inventory. And we sold out immediately! Everything was gone in the first week. Talk about God showing up and my mind being blown. As I look back, I do wish we had celebrated that first win in a very specific way. But we were just so amazed that it happened. I kept saying, "Wow, I really just sold one hundred bottles, and nobody knows anything about me." Our focus turned toward trying to sell the next hundred.

It wasn't long, however, before I realized we really weren't prepared for the kind of demand that was coming in. Nobody was. The manufacturer we initially partnered with did not expect us to take off the way we did. The lead time for the oil was already two weeks. When we sold out of everything, we didn't want to shut off the orders and lose momentum, so we kept the sales channels open despite the delays. Orders were starting to back up, and it was taking longer and longer to fulfill what was coming in. For some, this would have meant a quick end to a promising start. They would have given up, shut down, or carried on in the same way and ultimately lost customers because of poor service. Nope, not us. I refused to let this obstacle hinder something that clearly was having a positive impact on women across the country. We emailed our customers and communicated our progress with them via social media. We found a way to make it work.

As I've shared, Melvin played a crucial role in helping me manage the logistics. He'd worked tirelessly to build relationships with our manufacturer, so he kicked into gear when things looked bad. He basically got on the phone and said, "I don't care what you've got to do, but we can't have these people waiting this long for their orders. We're going to need you to expedite this manufacturing even if we've got to pay for it." Thankfully, we had substantial profit margins so we were able to reinvest that money into closing those lead times and doing more marketing.

Meanwhile, our basement became the hub of our operations. I handled the packaging and fulfillment myself. At one point, I was literally sterilizing the equipment, scooping product out of the large pails by hand, and filling each jar myself. Because the oil came already packaged and ready to ship, it was easier to fulfill those orders. But because we wanted to start developing more wet goods, we had a second product, the Babassu Deep Conditioner, that the manufacturer sent to us in large batches that needed to be transferred to pails. Then we still had to package that ourselves. This was done to cut the costs associated with having the manufacturer package it, but it was an incredibly tedious process.

Eventually, we scaled up for the very first—but certainly not the last—time. We moved from pails to fifty-five-gallon drums, and Melvin even built a contraption to pump the product from the drums into the bottles. No more scooping by hand, yay! Our setup wasn't glamorous, but it worked. We set up an assembly line in our basement with the help of family and friends—my mom, my neighbor, even one of my close friends, Charmane, pitched in to help us package and ship orders. Then, we scaled again. Quickly outgrowing the basement, we moved the operation to our garage. But even then, we were still fulfilling every order ourselves. It was all very labor-intensive, but it was what we had to do to get the product into the hands of our customers.

Said another way, I was tired! There were many days in those early years when I wasn't sure where I was going to find the strength to keep up the pace needed to grow a business that had come out of the gate on fire. I prayed and prayed that God would give me something to hold on to, something to keep me going. And He did. Every day, He renewed my strength. Every day, I learned more and more how to rely on Him.

The demands of starting a business or chasing a dream, especially when things are moving faster than you can keep up with, can be overwhelming. But if you trust in God and lean on Him no matter what, He will show up and lift you up, true to His Word in Isaiah 40:31, which promises, "But those who hope in the LORD will renew their strength. They will soar on wings like eagles; they will run and not grow weary; they will walk and not be faint." I clung to this when the workload felt impossible. Through it all, we kept going—and so can you! You don't have to have all the answers, but you should know how to find them.

> **When you stay focused on your vision and continue to share your journey with others, God's glory in your story will grow.**

When you stay focused on your vision and continue to share your journey with others, God's glory in your story will grow. Maybe I sound like a broken record at this point, but I can't say it enough: What sustained me through those long days and sleepless nights was my faith. The facts said we didn't have enough—enough time, resources, or energy. But my faith said we had an abundance. I trusted the Word when it said God would "meet all [my] needs according to the riches of his glory in Christ Jesus" (Philippians 4:19). That scripture reminded me that no matter how much I lacked, God's provision was more than enough. He would meet every need, whether that was providing the right connections, the finances to keep going, or the strength to push through the day-to-day grind.

———

Through this entire process, I was also balancing my role as a mother and wife. My daughters were four and eight years old when I started Mielle Organics, and I was determined to make sure they knew they were still the most important part of our lives. And I'm still like that today. I build my schedule based on what my girls have going on. That is very intentional, because I don't want my kids to grow resentful or feel like they come second to the business. I don't want them growing up and saying, "Well, you were never home. You were never here." So if I'm traveling, I try to take them with me as much as I can. I can't tell you how many times I'm at an event and someone will say, "Girl, you always got your kids."

You got that right.

I also make sure I'm always there for their activities. Out of, say, a hundred track or gymnastics meets my daughters might have over the course of a year, I'll probably attend ninety-five. And if I can't be there, someone from our family most definitely is. It is important to me that they see me as both a businesswoman and their mother.

I believe the idea of balance is really a false notion. Anytime you attempt to hold more than one role in life, something or someone will have to sacrifice to make it all happen. That's just the reality of being a working mother in America. The challenge is to make sure you remain in control of how much is sacrificed and to think of ways to make up for lost time. Over the years, there were certainly moments when it felt like too much to juggle mommying and Mielle.

Six months into the business, we secured our first photo shoot with a major influencer. It was truly a big deal and helped set the trajectory of establishing Mielle within the influencer community on social media. But this also meant I had to fly out on Halloween night for the November 1 shoot and miss taking my daughters trick-or-treating. I did everything I could to give them as much time as possible—including dressing them in their costumes and taking pictures with them before leaving. But I still had to go. Our neighbor took them instead.

It was one of those moments when I felt the weight of "mommy guilt" that I think every mom experiences when we have to make decisions that require our children to share us with a business or, for many high-profile people, the world. Nevertheless, I will never let mommy guilt take root inside of me. In every instance, I've chosen to remind myself of the bigger picture. I haven't built Mielle for just me. This has been as much about my family's future as it is about mine. If I had still been working as a nurse, I would have likely missed Halloween nights anyway, as I often had to work twelve-hour shifts on holidays. Now I have the privilege of making most of my girls' events, and if I do have to miss one, I can take some comfort in knowing that a photo shoot may lead to a major endorsement, which could lead to more exposure and sales, which could lead to greater part-nerships, which ultimately will lead to a life of greater opportunities for my girls. Thankfully, that's not something that happens much. I generally do everything I can to schedule my work around my girls' activities or take them with me on trips. I know God has called me to this work. And God also knows I have children. Because of this, God has a plan to make the scales divinely balance in a way they never could without Him at the helm of the vision.

———

When it comes to your business, it's going to take time to get that "balance" right. However long it takes, know that what's for you will not pass you. Also know that some seasons will be busier than others. Even though I've been intentional about making sure I'm present for my children, there was a season when I felt like I had to say yes to everything. This was especially true in the building stages of the business. I didn't have the privilege to say no to most things because it all felt important to our growth and the elevation of the brand. So I had to go to certain events. I had to take red-eye flights even though I hated them. I had to network despite my introverted tendencies. But the thing is, I knew that it was just a season I was in. I had no intention of making it the entirety of how I operated forever and ever. My yeses were going to eventually pay off and give me the privilege to say no when I really wanted to.

The hard part is, as an entrepreneur in the beauty industry, you never feel like your work is done. Even now, with the success Mielle has had, if I go somewhere and someone doesn't know the brand, I know there's more work to do.

I was just at the airport and a lady came up to me and said, "I love your hair. Your curls are so pretty. What do you use?" Of course, I asked, "Have you heard of Mielle?" The woman said, "No, I haven't heard of it." I turned to look at my daughter and said plainly, "I still have work to do."

You may be in a season where you have to say yes to a lot of things. I call that your grinding season. You may have to give away a lot of products. You may have to offer your services for free because you are building a reputation. You may have to lose some sleep to catch that red-eye back home so you can also be there for your children. In the midst of all that, still figure out how to be present, friend. Figure out how to prioritize what's important by having your support system or team carry some of the load so you can say yes or no accordingly.

And even in your beginning stages, practice saying no with small, low-stakes things. That way, you don't create such a habit of saying yes to everything that you can't brake it when you get to a cruising season or even a successful plateau—all because you've never done anything else. A great way to do this is to start with friends who might want more of your time and energy than you can give. They might not yet understand the sacrifices you're making. So the calls to go hang out or go shopping might be set aside so you can sit and do homework with your kids. Or return emails that you missed because you were going to one of your kids' sporting events. Practice telling others no. Get comfortable saying no so when you get the opportunity to say it to bigger, seemingly more important offers, no feels natural and familiar in your mouth.

———

Looking back on those early days, I realize that the willingness to start and the determination to keep going when things weren't going smoothly are the core reasons I've made it as far as I have. There were so many moments when we could have stopped, when it would have been easy to say, "This is too hard" or "We don't have enough." We could have let the rejections from manufacturers or the overwhelming demand after our launch slow us down, but we didn't. Instead, we took those challenges as opportunities to grow, to learn, and to push forward. And one thing I know for sure: If we can do it, so can you.

Beginnings don't dictate outcomes. You don't need to have all the resources or all the answers when you start—what you need is the willingness to keep going, even when it feels impossible. The journey is what shapes you, and the challenges you face along the way are what make the success that much sweeter. Every struggle, every no, every long night packaging orders in your basement may be part of God's plan to build something greater. It reminds me of James 1:2–4, which says, "Consider it pure joy, my brothers and sisters, whenever you face trials of many kinds, because you know that the testing of your faith produces perseverance. Let perseverance finish its work so that you may be mature and complete, not lacking anything." Each trial was molding me, strengthening my faith, and preparing me for the bigger blessings ahead.

For me and Melvin, Mielle was always about building something that would last, something that embodied the love and perseverance that has always been at the heart of our family. And none of it would have been possible if we hadn't decided to take that leap into the unknown and trust that we were capable of turning our dreams into reality. What we've built didn't happen overnight, and it didn't happen without sacrifice. But the triumphs we've experienced along the way have made every struggle worth it. We turned our grief into purpose, our challenges into opportunities, and our dreams into reality. And I believe anyone can do the same. You just need to take the first step.

QUESTIONS FOR REFLECTION

- Think about a goal or dream that you've been contemplating. What small step can you take today to move closer to making it a reality, even if you don't have all the resources or answers?
- Reflect on a time when you faced obstacles or rejections. How did you respond? What did you learn from that experience?

For My Family

7

Guiding Principle:
Choose legacy over everything.

THE ROLE OF FAMILY IN OUR LIVES, ESPECIALLY AS IT relates to success, cannot be overstated. For me, everything I do is driven by my daughters, Mia and Mackenzie. Mielle is their namesake, along with my son's.

I had Mia when I was twenty-two, and while that is young, I considered myself very mature for my age. I'd just graduated from a nursing program and begun my career at a local hospital. Melvin was working as an engineer at UPS. We were both hyper-focused on building our family and establishing ourselves as responsible people. As soon as Mia was born, I felt this intense and immediate desire to be the absolute best mother. More than anything, I didn't want her looking to the outside world for role models when she had me right there in front of her. That's what family means to me—being the foundation and example for those who come after me.

At the time, though, I didn't really think about my capital *P* Purpose. I had dreams, for sure. But my focus was more on what I needed to do to be the best mom I could be. The rest—ambition, building a business—came over time. That said, no matter what I did in business, I never wanted it to be about just me and my accomplishments. My intentions were to give my children something I didn't have growing up: stability and parents who had the capacity to be present and committed.

As a parent, it's easy to feel pressure from society—from people who think they know better about how you should raise your children, how you should build your career, or how you should balance both. But one thing I've learned is that no one outside of your home truly knows the full story. They don't see the sacrifices, the late nights, the quiet moments of self-doubt, or the overwhelming love that fuels you to keep going. That's why it's so important to stay focused on the people who matter most— your family. At the end of the day, their voices are the ones that should matter, not the voices of those who don't know you or understand your journey.

Melvin, Mia, and Mackenzie are the reason I push myself every day, and they are a constant reminder of why I have worked so hard to build something lasting. They are what keeps me grounded. But I've also come to realize that while family can be the greatest source of motivation, there is also so much that can happen to a family internally and externally to shift the focus away. That's why we need God. We need Him to guide us. To help us not allow those voices to drown out our purpose or impact the legacy we're building for our children.

———

Clearly, one of the most impactful turning points in my journey as a mother was the devastating loss of my son. Moving through that grief was the most challenging experience of my life. But even in that dark time, I tried to be strong for my daughters. I couldn't let them see me crumble. They needed to know that even in the face of immense pain, it was possible to find strength and hope. I wanted my girls to learn resilience, faith, and the power of perseverance through me, despite the fact that I was learning it in real time.

Children are incredibly perceptive. They are always paying attention. They absorb not just what we say but how we react to life's trials. What I didn't fully grasp at the time was just how closely the girls were watching. Maybe I should have realized since I was a very perceptive child myself, but grief can cloud your vision. Nevertheless, I'm grateful that my girls got a chance to see how we handled adversity, how we celebrated our wins, and how we picked ourselves up after a fall. I didn't realize it at the time, but when I was going through the toughest moment of my life, my daughters were quietly absorbing it all. Mia, especially, was soaking everything in. At eight years old, she was watching me grieve, yes, but she was also watching me grow closer to God. She had a front-row seat to the flourishing of my relationship with Him.

And it wasn't that we were constantly talking to Mia and her sister about our grief. We didn't talk to them about it much at all. We weren't sure that was the best thing for them since they were so young. I've always said that there is no proper way to grieve, and there is certainly no linear formula for moving through it. But the last thing we wanted was for our girls to feel the burden of carrying the weight of their parents' pain. Instead of involving them with things like the burial, we kept them away from those details and simply said in a way that a three- and eight-year-old could understand, "Your brother is in heaven. He's not coming home." I'm not sure that was the best way to approach it, but it made sense for us at the time.

Years after the loss of her brother, when Mia wrote her college essay, she chose to discuss that loss and how it shaped our family:

There were many nights I wondered why God would allow my brother to leave our family. Once the realization that my brother wasn't coming home set in, that is when things turned. My family, rocked by such a devastating bump in our life journey, began to recover. My parents, leading the way, modeled vulnerability and transparency. We spoke about grief, we checked on one another daily, and we never missed an opportunity to say *I love you!*

Looking back on that period of my life, I hadn't considered how much my brother's passing and its effect on my family helped mold me into who I am today. Back then, I was conditioned to believe that every question in life has an answer. Yet, that wasn't true in this case. Maybe an answer would have quelled the constant overthinking I did; however, it was in wrestling with my emotions and thoughts that growth took place.

I believe you are what you see, and my parents' example is one of struggle, fear, doubt, faith, love, and passion. Seeing this inspires me to wake up every morning, thanking God for another day and striving to be the best version of myself. I never thought I would feel gratitude for a loss, especially one of my younger brother. Yet, the lessons I have learned in life because of his passing have made me a better sister, daughter, and young woman.

Reading her essay was one of those light-bulb moments that had me saying to myself, *Oh, this is way bigger than me. This purpose is much bigger than what I can even imagine.* It was the first time I truly understood that she had witnessed me and Mel navigating our grief and leaning on our faith and each other. Our decision to press forward the way we did, leading to the creation of Mielle, had taught her invaluable lessons about not taking life for granted and embracing every opportunity. It was a revelation to learn the full extent of my influence on her, and I now understand just how my journey is intricately woven into both my girls and how my actions have far-reaching effects beyond what I can immediately see.

This realization reinforces my commitment to building a legacy—not just of financial success or business achievements, but of values, character, and faith. I want my daughters to inherit more than material wealth; I want them to inherit a rich legacy of integrity, compassion, and purpose.

There's a deep sense of responsibility that comes with being a parent and an entrepreneur. You're not just working for a paycheck or for personal accolades. You're working to create a foundation that your children can stand on. That's what legacy is about. It's about creating opportunities for those who come after you, so they don't have to struggle in the same ways you did.

And yet, if I'm honest with you, it's so easy to lose sight of that when the world around us is constantly telling us that we can't, or we shouldn't, or we're not enough. I can't recount how many times I've encountered naysayers on my journey. I'll talk about that in detail in a future chapter. But know this: People told me I wouldn't make it. They told me I didn't have what it takes to build a successful business. But every time those doubts crept in, I thought of my daughters. I knew I couldn't let the opinions of others dictate my path because I was building something bigger than myself, something for Mia and sister, and for future generations. And I refused to let outside voices tear that down.

> **You're not just working for a paycheck or for personal accolades. You're working to create a foundation that your children can stand on.**

As the girls grew older, I made a conscious effort to involve them in my work. I wanted them to feel like active participants in this journey, not passive observers. I took them on road trips, brought them to trade shows, and even had them work the cash register at events. Even though they were only in elementary school, they were engaging with customers, learning about entrepreneurship, and developing skills that would serve them throughout their lives. But involving my daughters in my work wasn't just about teaching them business skills; it was about showing them the importance of community service and hard work. It was about nurturing their character and helping them develop into compassionate, confident individuals who can make their own impact on the world. I wanted them to know that they've played a special role in creating and building this company. Because consequently, we have all had to make sacrifices. Sometimes that sacrifice was, "I've got to go out of town today. I won't be home tonight, sweetheart." That hurts a little less when you know your babies have been with you and seen what you do. When you know that they understand why Mommy has to leave for a day or two.

I also wanted them to know that this wasn't just Mommy and Daddy's dream. This dream was for them as well. It was their platform. With all the crawling and walking we had to do to build this, we hoped that when it was their time to pursue whatever dreams they may have, they'd be able to run toward them.

As I said, though, I am always careful not to impose my dreams onto them. I know firsthand the weight of expectations and the pressure that comes from trying to live up to someone else's vision of "good" and "worthy." God has ordained my girls with special gifts and talents. They have a purpose separate from what their parents have done with Mielle. I want Mia and Mackenzie to feel free to explore their own interests and passions, even if that means forging a completely different path from mine. That's why I'm not as interested in them taking over our business ventures as I am in wanting to know what they love, what they are passionate about. I ask them all the time, "How can Mommy support you and your dreams as you have supported Mommy through the years?" This has always been our dynamic, and now, with Mia, my oldest, I'm watching some of that pouring come full circle. She has gone off to college and is doing her own thing. My youngest also has her own thing going on. Neither is remotely interested in hair products. As I said, Mielle is simply the platform that will launch them into their greatest imaginations.

My goal has always been to provide my girls with the opportunities and resources that will afford them fewer obstacles than what their dad and I faced. But because I know I'm not the perfect parent and I'm not going to get everything right, I often check in with them. I will ask, "Am I doing a good job? Am I being a good mom? How do you feel? Do I spend enough time with you? Please tell me. I don't want you growing up wishing that I'd done or didn't do something. Tell me." Some days they don't have much to say, and I take that as a win. Other days, they are all in with their . . . feedback. That's a win too. Because while there's no playbook to being a good parent, having open dialogue and communication matters.

I guess at the core of it all, I want to break generational curses. I want the negative narratives of my childhood to end with me. I intend to create a new narrative for our family, one rooted in faith, love, and excellence. I know I'm planting seeds—seeds of wellness and faith that will grow into trees under whose shade I might never sit.

———

Keep in mind, family is not always those bound to you by blood. There are some of you who, for whatever reason, cannot imagine doing this kind of legacy building with your blood family. That's when having a chosen family matters. These are the people you meet along the way who become like brothers and sisters, mothers and fathers to you. The ones God has sent to love and care for you.

While I have solid relationships in my immediate family, I also have chosen family who are as much a part of what I've built as anyone else. One person is Germaine Bolds-Leftridge. Germaine was our very first sales broker at Mielle and was instrumental in helping to negotiate a deal with Sally Beauty Supply as well as all our other retail partners. But beyond being a savvy business exec, she has been an incredible source of wisdom. In many ways, Germaine has been a godmother figure in my life; I don't just go to her for business advice but also guidance for life and for my development as a woman.

She was the one who encouraged me as we entered major retail meetings. I tended to be quieter and more reserved. In fact, I was always a bit intimidated. I'd tell her, "What if these big retail chains don't get us? I don't know what to say. I don't know the language. I don't know what they want to hear." And Germaine would push me. She'd say, "You got this. You don't know you got it yet, but you got it. You don't know how powerful you are, but it's in you, Monique. It's in you." But she didn't just *say* those words. She also backed them up with action. She worked hard to help pull that *it*—confidence, owning my power—out of me. She never let me get in my own way by letting fear run things.

Your chosen family are the people around you who can silence the enemy. The enemy of impostor syndrome. The enemy of fear. The enemy of low self-worth. When I'd say, "Do I deserve to be here?" Germaine would say, "Girl, yes! These people are raving about Mielle. They love you." Having people around you like that—someone who is always there, always speaking life into you, but who is also not afraid to tell you the absolute truth—is everything.

Germaine was definitely not a "yes woman." She was a truth teller. In very loving ways, she wasn't afraid to tell me when I was wrong. She'd say, "Maybe you shouldn't have said it that way. Next time, try saying it this way." In fact, one of her favorite sayings was, "'Yes people' will get you killed." That always stuck with me because it's true. You don't want people telling you you're fine when the house is on fire. My legacy needs people to tell me the truth. That's the only way I can mature and blossom.

Another friend of mine, Marilyn, is also part of my chosen family. She's like my prayer warrior. I met her when I first started Mielle and she's always been very genuine. Our friendship has grown over the years, and I often call her my friend-therapist because every time I have an issue, I know I can go to her for sound advice. This is another instance of having someone in my life who will tell me the truth. I've said to her on many occasions, "Listen, if I'm wrong in this situation, please tell me I'm wrong. I want to know how to navigate and manage this from a biblical perspective." And that's exactly what she'll do. She'll not only pray for me but also offer good counsel.

Admittedly, I don't have a huge chosen family. I've unfortunately had too many people who were wolves in sheep's clothing. People who came into my life as supporters but who had other motives and agendas. So I treasure the circle of people who are close to me in this way. Like my family, they are the ones who give me the strength and determination to keep on keeping on. The number of people I consider to be chosen family might be small, but they are mighty.

Keeping God at the center has been the cornerstone of maintaining the strength of our family. Trusting in His plan, even when things don't make sense, has taught us patience and resilience. Even with family issues, I've learned that when I surrender my worries and stop trying to control every outcome, things often work out in ways I couldn't have imagined.

A recent experience with Mackenzie's schooling reinforced this lesson. We had been trying to get her into a particular private school for months. At one point, Melvin got really frustrated with the admissions officer, who, in hindsight, did seem to understand where we were coming from and why we were upset with the process. After more setbacks, I decided to journal and pray about it. It was time to release that thing to God because all the back-and-forth was driving me insane. In my journal, I wrote: *God, I pray that Mackenzie gets into the school; however, where You want her to be, it will work out for the good, and she will be where You have called her and assigned her to be.* Letting go of the stress of that process and trusting in God's plan brought me so much peace. And guess what? Favor won in the end. A few weeks later, we received the call that she had been accepted into the program. It was a powerful reminder for us both that when we let go and let God lead, things fall into place.

This principle applies not just to personal situations but to our larger goals and dreams. When we stay focused on our purpose and trust in the journey, we become less susceptible to the doubts and negativity that the world may project onto us. When we release our worries to God and trust in His perfect will for our lives, we can be assured that things will work out. Our faith and our family's support become the shield that protects our dreams.

When we stay focused on our purpose and trust in the journey, we become less susceptible to the doubts and negativity that the world may project onto us.

For me, instilling these kinds of values in our children is non-negotiable. And lecturing them won't work. Kids nowadays are savvy. They have the world at their fingertips and twenty-four-hour access to information. There are easily ten self-proclaimed gurus on TikTok right now talking about resilience or faith or purpose or legacy-building. But what kids don't always have are real-life demonstrations of that information. As the saying goes, "Some things are caught and not taught." As parents and as leaders, we have a responsibility to model the behaviors and attitudes we hope to see in our children. That means demonstrating integrity, kindness, and perseverance in the face of adversity. When we show our children what resilience looks like, then we inevitably teach them to stand strong in their own convictions. Every day we try to show Mia and Mackenzie that success isn't just about personal achievements but about contributing positively to the lives of others and building something that lasts.

It's important not to allow external negativity to infiltrate the sacred space of your family. In a world filled with noise and distractions, the family—the one we are born into or, for some of us, the one we create—serves as a grounding force. Family reminds us of why we started and who we're doing it for. As I said earlier, whenever I face challenges or feel overwhelmed, I look at my daughters and remember that every step I take is paving the way for them. Their futures, their opportunities, and their ability to dream without limits are what drive me to keep going. I encourage you to do the same. Maybe you don't have children. Maybe the legacy you leave will be for your nieces or nephews. Maybe it's for the students in your classroom or the neighborhood girls watching you drive by every day. Maybe you are leaving a lasting impression on the youth in your church or community organization. No matter what your legacy looks like, remember that someone is learning what's possible for themselves by watching you. And guess what? You might learn a little something in the process too.

That's what it all comes down to: growth. Growth for yourself, growth for your family, and growth for future generations. I often think about my future great-great-grandkids and how they will tell this story. I hope they will say, "I love being a part of this family because my great-great-grandmother and my great-great-granddad made a decision to know God and to serve Him. I come from people who carried a solid foundation of faith and passed that down from generation to generation. They followed their dreams and their passions, and that has created better opportunities for us. I want to be great and create Black excellence that continues their legacy."

I can't emphasize this enough: Every decision I make, every step I take in building this business, is with my family in mind. I want them to look back and see that we stood firm and didn't let the world deter us from God's purpose. If they *see* that, then I trust they'll *be* that.

QUESTIONS FOR REFLECTION

- Think about the legacy you want to leave behind for your loved ones. What values or principles do you want them to remember you for, and how can you start instilling those today?
- Now consider your current priorities. Are they aligned with the legacy you want to create for future generations? If not, what steps can you take to refocus on what truly matters?

The Art of Surrender

8

Guiding Principle:
Fear is real but it cannot drive.

FEAR HAS A STRANGE WAY OF SHOWING UP IN OUR lives right when we are on the cusp of something great—like becoming an entrepreneur. It's a sneaky thing, isn't it? The moment you decide to step into the unknown, fear rears its head, trying to force its way into the driver's seat. It's always in those critical moments—when you're standing at the edge, ready to take the leap—that fear starts to whisper in your ear, questioning whether you're capable, worthy, or even ready for what's to come. But if God gave it to you and has given you the go-ahead, then you are ready. The only real affirmation you need is God's Word. Right? Nevertheless, fear still barges in and fills our minds with doubt.

I've seen fear's powerful influence even in my own journey, particularly when I started Mielle. And what I've learned is that we can't force ourselves not to be afraid. It will show up. It's the way our bodies have learned to keep us safe and comfortable. But while fear is inevitable, we can still control it. If I've learned anything, it's this one important truth: Fear has no place dictating the decisions we make in business or life. In

Fear has no place dictating the decisions we make in business or life.

fact, fear should remain just what it is—a background player. It can observe from the sidelines, maybe even serve as a warning signal to help us discern who or what is operating in our best interest, but it should never take control of our lives. It's our faith that should be leading the charge.

As I reflect on the last decade of building my business, I notice that fear has shown up more times than I can count. Not only have I wrestled with the typical fears like the fear of failure, financial ruin, or public scrutiny—things every entrepreneur deals with at some point—but I've dealt with the fear of success itself. Why in the world would someone be afraid of success? Well, there's a kind of accountability that comes with godly success. And sometimes the weight of what's to come—the responsibilities, the expectations, the spotlight—can feel just as overwhelming as the fear of losing everything. There were many days in the early years of being an entrepreneur that I found myself wondering, *What if this works? What if this becomes bigger than I can handle? And even if I can handle it, can I maintain it?* There was this sense that I had to live up to the expectations that others placed upon me once they understood who I was and what I was trying to do with Mielle. And with that came a vulnerability that many people don't talk about. If I'd allowed that questioning of whether I was ready for the magnitude of what Mielle could be to take over, to rule me, then it's likely I would never have made the decisions necessary to grow the business to that point. If I had let my fear drive, it would have surely steered me off course.

I've run into countless aspiring entrepreneurs whom I can recognize immediately are allowing fear to control them. And the sad part is that they don't even realize it. Perhaps because sometimes fear will disguise itself as extreme practicality or caution. It's that voice that says, "Stay in your stable job," or "Don't take this risk because you might fail." And while there's absolutely a place for wisdom and careful planning, there's a difference between being cautious and being paralyzed. What too many people don't realize is that their fear, in many ways, isn't even their own. Many times, it's other people's worries and insecurities they are carrying. They've allowed others' fears to be projected onto their lives and prevent them from pursuing their dreams. My mother, for instance, was always concerned about stability. That was *her* experience based on *her* story. She couldn't understand why I would leave nursing—a stable, respectable career—to pursue a business that had no guarantees. But that's just it— she couldn't understand. And that's okay. I was never meant to carry her capacity to understand as my own. Even at a young age, when I wasn't so strongly rooted in my faith, I still walked to the beat of my own drum. I moved when I felt like moving and didn't allow her fears to stifle me. Especially in the ways it might have stifled her.

I've learned that fear can be generational. It's often passed down through our families, our communities, and our social circles. My mother's upbringing, for example, was rooted in survival. She had to make decisions based on necessity—doing whatever it took to put food on the table and maintain the security of her family. Her fear of instability was deeply ingrained, and it colored much of the unspoken advice I gleaned from her as I began my journey into entrepreneurship. My mother has a very persuasive way about her where she doesn't have to say, "Don't do this" or "Don't do that"; she just speaks as though her perspective is the only option. But while I completely understood where she was coming from, I wouldn't allow her fears to shape my path. Especially when I have my own fears to contend with.

That's another thing: Fear often disguises itself as wisdom from well-meaning people. My mother's advice came from a place of love, but it was still rooted in her fear. She had never taken the kinds of risks I was willing

Fear can be generational. It's often passed down through our families, our communities, and our social circles.

to take, and her advice reflected that. But as an entrepreneur, you have to be careful who you listen to. You can't take advice from people who haven't been where you're trying to go. Surround yourself with people who believe in your vision, who can offer support and encouragement, and who will help you stay grounded in your purpose.

As I've already made clear, I'm not immune to fear. I have plenty of my own fears. Some are clear-cut. I'm afraid of heights, snakes, and lizards, to name a few. Others are more deeply rooted in my childhood experiences and what I saw growing up. But somehow I knew very early on that if I wanted to live a different life from those around me, I had to steer my fear away from being the source of how I made decisions. And when I began my relationship with God, I realized that the only true way to do that was to feed my faith and starve my fear. As the saying goes, The thing you feed the longest grows the strongest. Everyone has some type of fear within them, but what is most important is how you manage it.

What do you choose to feed? When it comes to decisions that can change the trajectory of your life in a positive way, are you more willing to take the risk, feed your faith, and rise above your fears? I've realized that had I continued to feed the fears—generational or otherwise—that's what would be ever present in my life. When starting Mielle, I reminded myself of that repeatedly. Yes, it may seem easier to give up, to give in to the doubts, but don't let that be your portion. I knew I couldn't be the person God called me to be—the mother, the wife, the friend, the daughter, much less the business owner or philanthropist—if I allowed myself to be governed by fear. It's not easy, but over time we can decisively, regularly allow faith rather than fear to transform us, shape our character, and determine how we move through life.

Surround yourself with people who believe in your vision, who can offer support and encouragement, and who will help you stay grounded in your purpose.

One of the most damaging ways fear manifests is through negativity. People who allow fear to control them often end up with a negative outlook on life. I've seen this not just in business but in everyday interactions. Fear leads to doubt, and doubt breeds negativity. Negativity then becomes a breeding ground for stagnation. Think about it: People who constantly criticize others—whether online as internet trolls or in real life—are often driven by their own fears. They are sitting in their deep fear of change, success, and growth, and when they see someone else operating in faith, taking risks, and experiencing the fruit of those decisions, they become sullen or even angry. It then becomes easier for them to tear that person down rather than to confront their own insecurities.

I wish I could say that I've only observed this from a distance. That it's only been people in business or online or acquaintances who have succumbed to the projection of negativity in my life. Unfortunately, I've seen this dynamic play out even with those close to me. When I first started posting hair care recipes and tutorials online, people I considered friends questioned what I was doing. There were those who laughed at me, criticized my methods, and dismissed my vision. And because they were close to me, I could have taken it all to heart. But I refused to be swayed by the fear of what others may think of me and my ideas. So many people—myself included—hesitate to act because of the fear of being judged or ridiculed. I certainly could have embraced their criticism and decided that maybe I was on the wrong path. But I did not do that. I didn't let their opinions stop me. And that seemed to frustrate many of them. Mostly because my determination and persistence reflected back to them the gaps in their own ability to be determined and persistent.

When you believe in yourself and God's vision for your life, it shines a light on the fact that others do not believe in themselves or that God has a plan for their life. I imagine that is painful to feel. Maybe even embarrassing. But it's also none of my business. And when or if it happens to you, it's none of yours. Ironically, the same people who criticized me in the beginning eventually became the ones asking for my advice. They finally realized that their opinions said more about them than they did about me.

Sometimes I think the best entrepreneurs, the most successful ones, are those who are okay with looking stupid. Or with the potential to look stupid. And that can be tough, maybe even painful. But one's state of mind or level of belief in oneself surpasses any words someone else could say. Many of the same people who thought I was foolish for doing those live hair tutorials now see me as an authority. Yes, life can be hard; we just have to choose our hard. We can choose the hard of staying miserable in our job because we're scared to step out in faith and do what God has called us to do. Or we can choose the hard of taking a risk and pursuing our dream despite being criticized or not having the finances or support. Again, both scenarios are hard, but only one has the great reward of building our resilience and potentially letting God blow our mind with the fruit of our faith.

This doesn't mean we don't take good advice or counsel. Of course we do. I've done that many times over the course of my journey. But check that person's track record before you start internalizing what they are saying. Do they have experience in the field you're trying to go into? Have they built a business themselves? Do they have a level of authority and expertise to educate you on something? Because here's the thing: If you have not done or tried to do what I am doing, then your advice is probably not as solid and it's probably not coming from a place of wisdom. Which could also mean that God didn't send you to confirm or affirm a single thing about this vision He's given me.

Although it might sound harsh, sometimes ignorance is a choice. There's too much information available at your fingertips, too many people out there who have actually made their dreams come true and built businesses from nothing, for you to believe the first "I don't think you should do that" you hear from someone's mouth. We are all growing and, yes, we all make mistakes. But if you clearly see that a person is not qualified to give you any type of advice, and you choose to believe them anyway, you are operating from a posture of ignorance rather than enlightenment.

———

So yes, fear and negativity are closely intertwined, and they have a way of keeping people small. If you're not careful, fear will keep you from pursuing the life and business you're meant to have. When you surrender to fear, you stop moving forward. You become stuck in the same place, doing the same things, afraid of what might happen if you try something new. I'm not telling you to deny that you're scared. That's a natural human emotion. In fact, I'd go as far as to say that fear can often be a sign that you're on the right track. If you're not scared, you're probably not dreaming big enough—or you're relying on your own strength rather than God's. So acknowledge the fear but proceed anyhow.

When you surrender to fear, you stop moving forward.

Inevitably, I will get the question of how to distinguish between the kind of fear that keeps you stuck and the kind of fear that's a legitimate warning not to proceed. I personally believe these two feel different in the body. You can feel the difference between fear that arises because you are afraid of the unknown and fear that is a clear sign that you are going the wrong way. But a more tangible way to make the distinction is to spend time evaluating the true source of your vision or dream. This is where journaling comes in handy. Ask yourself, *Did God really give me that idea? Is this really my dream, or is it someone else's vision I'm trying to make happen? Has God sent something or someone to confirm this dream or to move me in the direction of this path?* You have to be honest with yourself. Is this business idea something you've been wanting so badly that you're telling yourself it's coming from God to force it to make sense? This is where having a prayer life and paying attention to your own life becomes necessary. It develops your intuition. If an idea, dream, or vision is from God, then He will affirm and confirm it. Doors will open. Though it may not always be easy, you will flow from one task to the next, even from one challenge to the next, with a bit more ease than if it's not from God. If you are doing something in your own strength, you'll likely find yourself in a perpetual state of frustration and overwhelm.

———

Entrepreneurship is one of the most fear-inducing paths you can take. It's not for the faint of heart. But the choice is yours: You can either let fear control you, or you can keep moving forward despite it. I chose to move forward, and it has made all the difference. Every major leap I've taken in my life and business has been accompanied by fear. It was there when I decided to quit nursing. It was there when I started my hair care line. It was there when I invested in scaling my business. But I didn't let it drive. Instead, I turned to God and surrendered those fears. Granted, surrender is a tricky thing. It's not about giving up control completely; it's about trusting that you don't need to be in control all the time. Surrender is saying, "I'm going to do my part, but I trust that God will handle the rest." That's what I did with Mielle.

In 2018, we went through significant financial hardships. I'll dig into the details later, but suffice it to say, we were growing rapidly, and while growth is a blessing, it comes with its own set of challenges. We found ourselves in a difficult position of needing more money, and instead of confronting the issues head-on, I got distracted. I started thinking about launching a fashion line with my mother, hoping it would bring in extra revenue to help with the company's financial issues. I kept telling myself that this would be a great way to give my fashionista mom something to do and to use my platform to help it grow.

Deep down, I knew good and well that this was not something I was supposed to be doing. God did *not* tell me to go start a fashion line. But I was using this "idea" as a distraction from the real problem. And, for a short time, I paid the price for it. We had such a hard time finding manufacturers and getting the line off the ground. Trying to launch that fashion line was stressful and took me away from the work that truly brought me joy—growing Mielle. It was clear. God was speaking. When I did something for the fashion line, I was exhausted and frustrated. But when I did something for Mielle, I was joyful. I was happy and energized.

So yes, maybe that's it too. Follow the joy. God is often found in the joy. The thing that genuinely makes you happy is most likely aligned with the path God wants you to take. And even if fear is present, it's likely not the kind that steals from you.

The same thing occurred when I tried to do online mentoring services. I created these courses for people who wanted one-on-one business mentorship to develop their personal brands. Although I love serving people, once again, this was not the route God told me to take. But I did it because it felt like the thing to do and I thought I could create another stream of revenue that would help the financial challenges Mielle was dealing with.

You can guess what happened.

People signed up. And after a while, my introverted self became completely drained. What was supposed to be business mentorship sessions became more like life coaching or therapy sessions and I was *not* equipped to be anyone's therapist. I could hear God speaking again: *This is not your call. This is not for you.*

When you're out of alignment but you have a relationship with God, you will quickly decipher your wrong turns, and hopefully—if you don't let pride get in the way—you'll get back on the right road. That's exactly what I did. I shut down both the fashion line and the mentoring services and focused my attention on Mielle.

I challenge you to ask yourself if that thing you are wanting to do is in alignment with what God has confirmed all around you. Do you have peace about it? Is there some degree of calm, even if there are challenges or bumps in the road? Here's the valuable lesson I got from that experience: You can't run away from fear. But you also can't "deal with it" by picking up any and every distraction in order to convince yourself you are handling things well. Instead, you must surrender the fear and be still enough to hear God's plan for your next move. That's what releasing the fear looks like. It doesn't always look like rushing to concoct a plan to fix the problem you think you have because you're afraid. Rather, it looks like getting quiet and waiting for instructions from the one who can see the future. When I finally surrendered to God's plan for Mielle, things started to turn around. We found our footing again and continued to grow. That was God's plan all along. But I had to let go of my need to control everything, my desire to fix my fear, before He could step in.

Now, I'm pretty sure that, at the time, I didn't see any of this as "surrendering." We tend to think of surrender in overtly spiritual terms. But really, surrendering is simply about letting go. Taking our hands off the wheel. I said, "I'm letting this fashion line go so I can get back on track. God will provide a way of escape."

And He did. Mielle is still here. You see, when your hands are all in that thing you said God gave you, He will take a step back and wait for you to finish doing you. God is not going to force our obedience. But the outcome of our need to be in control will be evident. And once we let go of that thing and invite God to take over, He will absolutely come in and do what *He* does. When we let go, God takes over, and blessings are inevitable.

There's a reason the Bible reminds us that God did not give us a spirit of fear, but of power, love, and a sound mind (2 Timothy 1:7). Fear is natural to us as humans, but it doesn't move God. And because it doesn't override the power, love, and sound mind God has given us, it has no place in the decisions we make. I firmly believe that if God gave me a sound mind, then I'm going to question those fearful thoughts every time they arise.

If you feel as though you are being sidetracked by fear, ask yourself, *Where are these thoughts coming from? Are they in alignment with the sound mind God promised me?* Then check to see if there is anything you are doing to fuel that fear. Has somebody projected their fear onto you and you've just absorbed it? Are you watching too much news? Are you consuming too much on social media? Are you watching the wrong movies, listening to the wrong music or podcasts, reading the wrong books? I believe that our eyes and ears are the gateway to our souls, so it's important to check the source of our fears. If we can't truly validate the fear we feel, and it doesn't align with what the Word of God says or what the Holy Spirit has spoken to us, then it must be silenced. It must be starved of attention.

However, just like most enemies of our growth, fear is persistent. It will always try to find a way in, especially when we're on the verge of something great. But it's never going to be the thing God uses to move us forward. Fear, in the end, is just a background player in our lives. As entrepreneurs, as dreamers, we must always keep our eyes on the bigger picture. Fear will always be there, but it doesn't have the final say in the big decisions. We do. If we let it, fear will keep us small, stuck, and stagnant. Let's not accept that. Let's lead with our faith.

> **Fear will always be there, but it doesn't have the final say in the big decisions.**

QUESTIONS FOR REFLECTION

- What has fear prevented you from pursuing that you feel called to do? What would it look like for you to take that first step today, despite the fear?

- Consider a current situation in your life where you feel the need to control the outcome. What might it look like to surrender that control and trust that things will work out in the way they're meant to?

Trust the Process

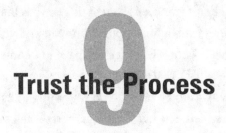

Guiding Principle:
Don't just survive—thrive.

WHEN GOD GIVES YOU A VISION, HE DOESN'T JUST give it to you. I believe He gives a particular idea to many people because He knows just how creative and ingenious He's made us. But I also believe that the level of success we experience when it comes to bringing an idea or vision to life is directly related to our obedience. God is waiting to see who will be obedient to His call. Who will pay close attention to how and where He is leading them.

There were plenty of other businesses creating and selling natural hair products when I started Mielle. I wasn't reinventing the wheel as much as being obedient at every step of the journey as God guided me toward a larger dream He had for me. One I couldn't have even imagined at the time when I was simply surviving as an entrepreneur. God was preparing me to thrive but wanted to make sure I would follow His voice.

This reminds me of the story of Esther in the Bible, who at first glance seemed destined to only serve in the harem of King Xerxes' court. But God chose her to become queen of Persia and to save the Jewish people—her people—who were being held in captivity. When Esther questioned God's prophet and her cousin, Mordecai, about this—uncertain as to whether she was fit to be the one to approach the king—Mordecai said, "Do not think to yourself that in the king's palace you will escape any more than all the other Jews. For if you keep silent at this time, relief and deliverance will rise for the Jews from another place, but you and your father's house will perish. And who knows whether you have not come to the kingdom for such a time as this?" (Esther 4:13–14 ESV). Did you catch that? The destiny of the Jews was to be saved. God was going to use someone to do it. He called Esther, and she eventually gathered the courage to answer, knowing that if she didn't, she, her family, and many of her people would die. However, God would have still accomplished His purpose whether she answered the call or not.

This is what we must remember when we find ourselves hedging on a dream, vision, or idea God has given us. Being in constant survival mode early in one's entrepreneurial journey—worried about the next dollar or how the next product will get made or what that other company in the same industry is doing—can often muddle your vision, narrow your capacity, and cause you to forget that God might be using you to accomplish a greater plan. A plan that will come to pass regardless of whether you accept your role in it. To thrive, we must choose to see the bigger picture and be willing to say, "Yes, God!" no matter what our circumstances look like.

Thriving, for me, has never been just about building a successful business—it's about finding balance and joy in every area of my life, including the personal. One way I see myself thriving now is through the household I've created for my family. It's not perfect—we have our disagreements and misunderstandings—but I've been intentional about building a home that represents peace. My family and I choose to communicate with each other even when things are hard. We've worked to create an environment where we can talk openly, listen to one another, and work through challenges together. That kind of safe space is something I take pride in and something I know God is pleased with.

The story of Esther resonates with me because, even as a teenager, I felt called to be an entrepreneur. The pull on my heart and mind to have my own business, control my own schedule, and make my own money was strong. And as I've shared, I answered the call many times before starting Mielle. Even when the multilevel marketing opportunities didn't pan out and I decided to root myself in the medical field as a nurse, I was still thinking with that entrepreneurial brain of mine. I even wrote a business plan to start a nursing agency, thinking I could combine all my skills into my business.

God blocked that too.

See, this is what happens when you are just going through your days, not listening closely to the details of the vision God placed deep down in your heart, or worse, deciding that you know how to execute that vision on your own. That resistance will have you in constant search mode with faulty motivations. You'll find yourself trying all kinds of things, hoping that you will get to some arbitrary million-dollar end goal. Not realizing that the dream God gave you could be worth one hundred million dollars. Trying to do it on your own doesn't mean you won't be able to have and grow that dream. It absolutely does mean that you will end up selling yourself short.

Thankfully, though, God doesn't throw His people away. Even when we wander from the path, God is so good that He will use what we've learned in our searching to help guide us back on the path. But it's still up to us to be open to the process, whatever it might look like. I encourage you to not settle for something "pretty good" when God has something great on the other side of your process.

I had a deep soul-level awareness that I was called to be an entrepreneur. But because I didn't have a close relationship with God at the time, I had no way of following more purposeful paths. Though I spent many years trying things, I never could pinpoint what I truly loved and was passionate about, despite my love of hair and beauty staring me in the face. All those "tries" never took off because I wasn't clear on God's purpose for me being in business for myself. I was chasing money, trying to become a millionaire, and looking for an escape from nursing. But I wasn't doing anything that was rooted in my passion and that served others.

But as I said, the beautiful thing about God is that He will use it all. He allowed me the space to try many different business opportunities so I could ultimately discover who I was and what worked best for me. When I finally got what I needed, He made sure that nothing else would work until my relationship with Him was solidified and the dream became clear. And when I say nothing else would work, I mean *nothing*. After my various attempts at entrepreneurship didn't take off, I went back to school to become a nurse practitioner—twice. The first time, in the middle of the semester, I got pregnant with Mackenzie, who ended up being born prematurely. So of course I dropped out to focus on her health. Three years later, I went back to school. But as soon as I enrolled, I found out I was pregnant with my son. So, I dropped out again.

Clearly, I was not supposed to become a nurse practitioner.

Okay, God . . . so how do You want to use me? What is the plan?

Ah, now I was getting somewhere. There's something about that kind of surrender. That willingness to ask God for His guidance. It can be hard to get there sometimes. If you have an entrepreneur's mind, it can be easy to simply move on to the next hustle, the next grind. You become used to doing it all yourself and develop a pattern of ignoring the voice of God when He speaks. The thing is, when God calls you to do something and you ignore that call, He will absolutely get your attention. I couldn't have started Mielle until *after* I began grieving. *After* turning my life over to God. Again, I don't believe God orchestrated my loss, but I do believe He used the stillness that the loss created to speak to my heart. In those six months my son spent in the NICU fighting for his life, I finally admitted to myself and to God that I could not figure life out on my own. I needed God no matter what happened. *We* needed Him. Everything shifted after we accepted Jesus as our Lord and Savior.

Yes, we still lost our son. But though he was here for a short time, his life was purpose-driven. His presence drove us back to God, and with God we were about to thrive in a way we never had before. In the months after Milan's passing, God gave me a vision to serve women through beauty. But I was still working through what that would look like. As I mentioned earlier, my initial idea was to open a hair salon. I wanted to create an atmosphere where women could feel safe and appreciated while getting their hair done. Writing the business plan for the salon grounded me when grief tried to take me out. But ultimately, the salon was simply an idea that would get me on a path to the true vision.

After finishing my salon business plan, I attended a branding workshop and spoke about my idea with the presenter, Angela C. Styles, a renowned hair stylist and salon owner. She was clearly impressed with my creativity and business sense and told me as much.

"But you're a nurse, right?" she asked.

"Yes."

"Hmm, okay. Well, you can definitely do this. You have what it takes. I just don't know if you're going to get the respect from other hairstylists. There are so many personalities in this business. It may be a little challenging to operate a salon when you don't really do hair."

I had never thought of it that way and realized this introvert wanted no part of that potential drama!

Some people might think, *Oh, she was a hater. She just didn't want you to pursue your dream.* But I was discerning enough at the time to realize that not everyone is a hater. It was simply good advice, given with great compassion, from someone who knew the business better than I did.

So I revised my plan to focus on hair products that I could sell to salons and consumers. First, I planned to develop a hair vitamin. This felt like a great way to use my nursing background to educate women on healthy development and growth. Still, I didn't move on the hair vitamin at first. I simply kept it in the back of my mind and continued trying to figure out how I would bring products to life with no chemist and very few resources. And while I was in survival mode, the clock was ticking on my idea.

As I was researching on the internet and perusing the pages of smaller beauty brands on social media, I saw that there were several hair vitamins on the market. Interestingly enough, I didn't see the other hair vitamin companies as competition. I just viewed them as the push I needed to get going on the vision God had put in my head.

God wants to use you. He wants to use your creativity and gifts to serve the world. But guess what? He also wants to use them for your benefit! There's healing in allowing ourselves to be vessels for God's work on earth. There's joy in activating our gifts for the purposes of God. When we don't act on all the signs He sends our way, not only will we find ourselves watching our visions come to pass elsewhere, but we will also miss out on the restoration that comes with obeying God.

Back then, I could never have dreamed of the life I have now. Not in a million years. Growing up, I imagined my life as stable and predictable— exactly what I know my mom hoped for when she'd say, "I want you to be better than me." For me, that translated into going to college, getting a degree, and building a career with job security, a good salary, and a solid 401(k) account. That was my plan: a straightforward life that checked all the boxes. But looking back, I realize that while that might have been a good life, it wasn't the life God had for me. I spent many years in survival mode trying to make it happen. That is, until I began to trust God and the process He was taking me through and all the ways He was refining me. By surrendering my limited imagination, I learned to simply listen to Him. And when it came to my business, I refused to sit on the sidelines and watch someone else pursue what I aspired to do. It was time to find the courage of Esther, step out of my comfort zone, and take the risk. Those other hair vitamin products were just another reminder that God gives a vision to multiple people. If you don't act on that dream He has placed in your heart, He will absolutely find someone else to do it. So I did. I created my product and put it out into the world.

But I didn't stop there.

I had to believe that what God had given me was real and worth pursuing. And the only way I could do that was by putting my words to action. That was the hard part. It required me to get comfortable with rejection and trust the process.

There were many times when I cold-called social media influencers to promote my product and got no response. I would obtain their emails from their bios on Instagram and send them a message saying, "Hey, I'm starting a new company. It's a Black-owned natural hair products business that uses natural ingredients. I would love to send you a package." Now, I will admit, I didn't know anything about how influencers worked at the time. I had no idea that the top beauty influencers were being paid to promote brands. I just thought they were sent packages and then gave their opinion on the products. I had much to learn about the business, and rejection was ready and willing to teach me.

There was one influencer I reached out to who was very popular in the natural hair community. I was so excited when she agreed to check out my products and gave me her address to send our package.

"Oh my goodness! This is so great!" I told Melvin. "She's going to try my product and post about it. I'm going to get a lot of views and followers from that."

Well, unfortunately, that's not quite what happened. The influencer actually sent the product back. She even took the time to handwrite "Return to sender" on the package. I was stunned.

At first, I thought maybe it was a mistake. So I emailed the influencer and asked her why she sent the product back.

"Weren't you interested in using and reviewing the product?" I asked.

She responded quickly. "Oh, I'm sorry. This brand does not align with my personal brand, so I cannot post or talk about the product."

What does that even mean?

That was it. Let me tell you, my feelings were so hurt. I almost would have preferred that she threw the product away and ghosted me on the review. Receiving it back created so much anxiety for me and, for a little while, affected my confidence. I found myself questioning everything.

What was really wrong with the product?

Is the packaging not good enough?

The pain that comes with rejection is very real, and I took this one hard. I know now that some of my reaction was related to my unhealed childhood trauma. When the influencer said no, it triggered feelings I'd long had of not feeling seen. Her rejection sounded like the voices of those family members who had already named me as a failure before I'd even had a chance to show that I could succeed.

There was something deep down in me, though, that would not give up. Despite feeling bad about the influencer's response, I kept going. It was one of those moments when I'd decided to throw in the towel, only to have God throw it right back at me. It was like the Holy Spirit was whispering in my ear: *Pick yourself up. Give those tears to Me. Don't be anxious. Don't be afraid. I got you.*

That experience was the first time I learned an entrepreneurial lesson that has never left me: If you get a no, that just means you haven't talked to the right person yet. If you keep knocking on doors, somebody is going to answer eventually.

As I worried about what one person's rejection might say about my product or, worse, about me, I could have retreated, gone into survival mode, or even quit. But the one thing I was sure of was that God didn't give me this vision to leave me. I knew that as long as I remained faithful to this dream, He would remain faithful to helping it come to pass. So I chose to listen to my faith rather than the negative voices. Thriving only comes to those who persist. You must keep going even when those voices are loud. Whether you are an entrepreneur or pursuing a different kind of dream, you must keep believing in yourself and what you are trying to do. I kept believing in my product and kept reaching out to influencers until I found success. It wasn't too long after that terrible rejection that my persistence paid off and a major influencer agreed to promote my product.

There was another significant moment in my entrepreneurial journey that required me to trust God's process. This time, it was when we decided to bring Mielle into the retail space. That was truly a leap of faith. When Sally Beauty approached us in 2015, we had no experience with large retailers whatsoever. But again, I decided to trust that God would lead us through the process. Listen, my friend. It was such a moment of alignment.

When we got the call for a meeting with Sally's executives, we were actually in Dallas, Texas, for Mia's gymnastics competition, just a short drive from their headquarters. We were so nervous about this meeting, and we also had no babysitter for our children. We didn't know anyone in Texas, and we had initially only planned to be there for the competition. The first inkling we had that this might be a God-ordained partnership with Sally was when we received this response: "Bring your daughters to the meeting. It's okay. They can come."

Wow! Our girls were five and nine at the time, so this was a huge deal.

"You all better be quiet," I said. "This is a great opportunity for Mommy."

Melvin and I showed up with no formal presentation—just our babies and our integrity—but it turned out that we had nothing to worry about. The meeting went great. They were so excited to hear us talk about the company because they'd heard about all the momentum we were building on social media.

"We want to test Mielle in ninety-five stores. We'll see how you do and go from there."

Again, a huge deal! And an even bigger test.

I suppose I could have thought about all the rejections from the past. I could have allowed my confidence to remain shot and tell them we'd think about it. But there was no way I was doing that. I had God on my side, and I was going to move forward.

And we did it! We launched in Sally Beauty that following February and sold out in every single one of those ninety-five stores in less than two hours. It was something they'd never seen before. It got to the point that, after posting about which stores we were in, customers began bugging the store managers for products, and the CEO of Sally Beauty told us to slow down on our social media promotions.

My response? "We just posted that we were in ninety-five stores. That's what you asked us to do. This is nothing but God doing all of this, so you've got to take that up with Him, not me."

Still trusting You, Father.

This leap of faith led to our expansion into other retailers like Target. Finally, we were offered an opportunity of a lifetime to play with the big dogs. The question now was, Could we still hear God and do the next right thing for *this* dream?

When Walmart came calling, we had another huge decision to make. One that required us to trust God with our business like nothing else up to that point. Walmart was the biggest brick-and-mortar retailer in the world, and they were interested in carrying Mielle. It seemed like a no-brainer at first. But we also knew that if we messed up with them, there was no going back. We wouldn't likely get a second shot. So after much discussion—and maybe a little fretting—we turned Walmart down.

This is such a huge lesson for an entrepreneur. Because when you have something you've created and your dream is to be a global sensation, and you get a call from the biggest retailer in the world, it can be incredibly easy to dive headfirst into that opportunity without considering whether you are truly ready to handle all that comes with it. For Mielle to operate at that scale, more was going to be required of us that we did not yet have. So I had to set my emotions aside, put on my CEO hat, gather my team, and ask the hard questions: Infrastructure-wise, are we ready to go into Walmart? What will this look like if we do get in and can't meet the orders?

This wasn't an easy decision. All my competitors were going into Walmart, left and right. And many were doing very well there. The temptation to leap was very present, and I'm certain there were people who thought that not doing this deal immediately demonstrated our lack of faith. That was certainly not the case. I urge you to be careful about attaching God to decisions that are very much your own manipulations and are rooted in your desire to do what everyone else is doing and not what He's put on your path. I knew what my gut was telling me. What God was saying. *It wasn't time yet.*

Do not compare your dream, your journey, your chapter to someone else's. In every area of life, but especially in business, you must stay focused. Stay in your lane. Our motto was always "Slow and steady wins the race." When you go slow and you're not trying to compete, you can really focus on the business in front of you.

Do not compare your dream, your journey, your chapter to someone else's.

It took a lot of trust, but I knew that what God had for us—for Mielle—was not going to pass us up. If we truly believed our brand was as good as we said it was, if we knew that our customers loved us, then we could take the time to continue building infrastructure, hiring the right people, creating the necessary resources, and ultimately scaling this company. And that's what we did.

And guess who was knocking on our door the following year?

Exactly!

Our first products entered Walmart the next year *after* killing it in Sally Beauty and Target. And *after* continuing to build our customer base. Although we are the founders, our customers are our bosses and we do what they say. When we did go into Walmart, we had grown the business to the point where we could stay there.

Part of trusting the process means staying true to the vision God has given you as well as the blueprint for that vision. God wanted us to run our business a particular way, which meant that we would not necessarily be able to jump when others jumped or walk away when others walked away. Having the business model of "slow and steady" required us to keep our eyes on the bigger picture, the bigger promise.

Friend, trusting God sometimes involves more than we are led to believe by even the best of believers. Yes, it's important to pray. Prayer is absolutely the way we communicate our desires and needs and frustrations to God. If you're not praying about decisions, if you're not asking God for direction, then there's no way to know what to do next.

My favorite way to pray is through journaling. I believe there is power in writing the vision and making it plain (Habakkuk 2:2). There have been many moments when I've seen prayers written years prior answered right before my eyes. Sometimes at the end of a journaling session, I'll ask God, "What do I do with this?" and on many occasions He has answered.

Beyond praying, part of hearing God has been paying attention to my body. God created us with a central nervous system that will speak to us if we listen. God is not a God of chaos and confusion. He does not want us to be indecisive. So when I begin to feel confused about something to which God might be telling me no, I feel it. There's an unsettledness in my stomach. Or a sensation in my chest. I don't feel ease or peace. But when I make decisions and that warm sensation of peace comes over me, that is my confirmation. God is telling me to proceed.

Of course, I'm not perfect. I've made many mistakes. Which is why I'm so thankful for the grace of God. First Corinthians 10:13 says that God is faithful and will always "provide the way of escape" (ESV). So even if I get rerouted, head in the wrong direction, or am tempted to follow the crowd, I'm not going to stay on that path long because God will reroute me and put me back in alignment with His will if I continue to listen. As long as I continue to pay attention, may His will be done.

Ultimately, we have to be willing to let God do His work. Some of us pray and then get in the way. We pray, then spend weeks worrying about what we prayed for. Trusting God's process means not worrying and stressing about the outcomes. If that thing (whatever that thing is) is God's will for you, then work toward letting the anxiety go. Worrying only leads us to try to orchestrate an outcome ourselves. Take your hands off it, and trust that God is working it out in the background for your good. That ability to surrender and say, "If God wants us in Walmart, we'll be there when we're ready," or "If that influencer is supposed to promote our products, then they will" is so liberating. All God is asking for us to do is pray and do the work He has called us to. Leave the outcomes to Him, and trust that He will always provide "exceedingly abundantly above all that [you] ask or think" (Ephesians 3:20 NKJV). Of course, this charge to trust God applies even when our circumstances are less than ideal.

As 2018 rolled over into the new year, we began to see a big hole in Mielle's financials. We were growing steadily, but transitioning from direct sales to retail sales can be very expensive. You can end up spending millions in marketing. In addition, we had the wrong people handling our books. The accountant we had at the time didn't understand our business and, we later learned, was not handling our finances well. In short, they didn't understand how our industry worked and weren't booking the trade marketing dollars we were supposed to be spending with our retail partners, so we ended up having less for marketing than we anticipated. As a result, we were $2 million in the hole.

Trusting God's process means not worrying and stressing about the outcomes.

To fix this, we did what most business owners try to do. We went to the banks. As you might expect, nearly every bank we went to said no. One bank did offer us a line of credit, which we took, but, again, being new to doing business at this level, we didn't realize that the line of credit should have been used to finance inventory and not marketing. Because of that, the bank was not happy and called our line of credit due because it wasn't being paid down fast enough. Of course, when they called it due, we didn't have the money because we'd spent it already.

Things got scary very quickly. When you are a small business, most banks require a personal guarantee. So when the line of credit came due, the banks basically said, "If you don't pay this, next in line is your house. We're going to take your home." That's when everything got crystal clear for me. I didn't know if Mielle was going to survive. I didn't know if we were going to make it through this hard season. But I knew we had to keep going. We had to try to figure this out.

So despite what was going on, I showed up at the office every day with a smile on my face. We paid our employees even when we couldn't pay ourselves. I still came to meetings, still engaged with my employees, all as if nothing was wrong. And I was on my face every night, praying to God to help us weather this storm.

Father, You have to work this out.

We finally came to terms with the fact that we were going to have to take on an investor—a process that was surely going to require more faith, more trust.

One of our first conversations was with a small investment company that had experience in the beauty industry and was very interested in investing in us because, on the surface, we were still growing. Yes, our back end was in shambles, but Mielle was still moving more and more products, and the brand was doing amazing. If I'm honest, *that* was our entire pitch. We basically said to these potential partners, "We know the numbers look awful. But look how the brand is performing. Can you even imagine what an infusion of cash, managed well, might do?" Because listen . . . I still believed in Mielle. I believed that God would not have the brand performing this well if He wasn't going to continue to carry us through. And the investment company thought so too. So much so that they recommended we first bring on their CFO as a consultant to help us organize our books, which were, as you might imagine, all over the place. An older man who had been retired for many years and served at the firm as a consultant despite what the title suggested, the CFO took a liking to us and spent hours organizing the books and coaching us. We were so grateful when he finished and gave our company the thumbs-up about our progress. "You all should definitely invest in them," he told them. "They're a really great couple. Just needed a little help."

Fantastic, right?

Well, I suppose every story must have a twist here or a turn there before it arrives at a satisfactory ending. This is no different. After the CFO affirmed our business as a great candidate for investment, there was a lot of back-and-forth with the company. They'd express excitement one day, and then days later pull back. They'd say, "We're almost there" in one conversation and then, "Well, we want to check one more thing" in another. Even the CFO was upset. "They're playing games. I don't understand why they won't just write the check and invest in you. You've done the work."

Meanwhile, our company was still in trouble. Our house was still at risk of being taken. It was six months of an emotional roller coaster as we tried to do everything possible to keep the business afloat.

Trust the process.

Trust the process.

Trust the process.

Finally, they came back with an offer. They were going to give us the $2 million we needed to get out of the hole, but they wanted 40 percent of the company.

Wait, what?

Sometimes you just know. Remember when I said that God has built an alarm system in your body called the central nervous system? Your body and spirit will let you know when something isn't right. God will cause an uneasiness in your spirit even before things go completely left. These people had become cold in their conversations with us. With every new discussion, they were less warm and friendly. Except for the CFO, our personalities didn't mesh well at all. I was already apprehensive, so the request for nearly half our company felt like a huge red flag.

But even then, with all that information, we still considered the deal. Because at the end of the day, we needed the money if there was any hope for Mielle to survive. After a couple of weeks of Melvin and me going back and forth with each other on whether to take the deal, the investment company contacted us and did a complete one-eighty. They retracted the offer.

"You know what? We're actually not going to be able to invest in you, because we think you guys still need to clean up your books more. We're going to recommend someone outside of our CFO to help get you in a position where you're more financially stable before we make an investment in you."

We were beyond shocked. Melvin was livid and told them as much. They knew the bank was breathing down our necks. They knew all that we were going through and still strung us along, only to walk out on us at the last hour. Even their CFO, who'd worked diligently with and for us, was angry. He ultimately ended up leaving that firm to come work for us full-time as our CFO.

But let me tell you, God is always present. He is always there, guiding and soothing and letting you know what the next move should be. The whole time my husband was very sternly but professionally letting the investors have a piece of his mind on the phone, I sat there quietly. The only way I can explain it is that as he was talking, I felt an overwhelming calm wash over me. Yes, we needed the money. No, we didn't know what we were going to do next. But I had a deep sense of peace. God didn't want us to work with that other company. But Mielle was not going to go under. He was going to work it out.

God is always present. He is always there, guiding and soothing and letting you know what the next move should be.

And He did. In a way that still blows my mind. But more on that later.

We certainly could have given up. We could have tried to liquidate our inventory and walked away from the business we'd poured our heart and soul into. But that was not an option. We ultimately decided to stay the course and trust that even this bump in the road would lead to God's favor with the right investors who would have more favorable terms to help turn the company around.

But even if we didn't eventually land an investor, this situation taught us so much professionally and personally. More than anything, it brought us closer to God. It taught us the true meaning of surrender. Friend, surrendering to God's process—whatever that might look like—opens the door for God to say, "Okay, bet. She's obedient. He's trusting Me. They don't have their hands on it. Let Me do My thing." Trusting God's process, even if it means letting go of what you thought success looked like, is the key to any kind of growth, business or otherwise. It's not just about believing in God. It's about being willing to let go of our very finite understanding of the way things are supposed to be and allowing God to work on our behalf and beyond our expectations, fulfilling His plans for us in ways we could never imagine.

QUESTIONS FOR REFLECTION

- Think about a time when you received advice that didn't align with your vision. How did you discern what to take on board versus what to let go of, and what was the outcome?
- Describe an area in your life right now where you feel uncertain or afraid to move forward. How can you invite God into that situation and trust the process, even when the outcome isn't clear?

To Go Far, Go Together

Guiding Principle:
Collaboration will get you everywhere.

PARTNERSHIPS AND COLLABORATIONS HAVE BEEN AT the core of every success I've experienced, whether in business or in my personal life. But the deeper I dive into these relationships, the more I recognize that at the heart of every strong collaboration is trust. Most important to me is trusting God to bring about the blessings and lessons through my experiences. And through His guidance, I've grown the ability to trust my own decision-making, which includes partnering with the right people and organizations. When I think about what it takes to truly and freely collaborate with someone, whether it's my husband or a business partner, I realize it starts with deep trust.

God didn't create us to walk this journey alone. He designed us for relationships, for community. And with community comes collaboration. Even in Genesis, we see that Adam wasn't meant to be alone. God created Eve not just to be his companion but his partner. We were created to support and uplift one another, and to walk through life's challenges together. In both my business and personal life, my most fruitful collaborations

> God didn't create us to walk this journey alone. He designed us for relationships, for community.

have been the ones where both parties understand this divine purpose.

I've always said that there is strength in numbers. I love the African proverb that says, "If you want to go fast, go alone. If you want to go far, go together." I'm one CEO. It's impossible for me to know everything. It's our job as people and especially as leaders to find and build community.

This is why we're here, why we were created! Even God's Word talks about the power of community. "For where two or three are gathered together in my name, there am I among them" (Matthew 18:20 ESV). God wants us to be together and to do things with other like-minded believers. And "like-minded" really is the key here. I work with all kinds of people and have done so successfully. But when you work with someone who is also a believer and you share the same vision and similar goals, you can go far together.

To be clear, I don't necessarily get in the weeds about what denomination a person belongs to or even what religion someone practices. Not when I'm considering a collaboration in business, at least. But I do love working with someone who outwardly expresses a belief in God, because it's easy for me to see in that person a personal conviction and a moral compass. There's something greater guiding their integrity and principles. If you are simply living within your own power without any belief system, well, that's hard for me to trust. Though it's sometimes unavoidable at the levels of business I've reached to always work with a person or entity who believes in God, it's still an ideal that's important to me. And even if I'm not working with a believer, it's very clear that I am one. I try to ensure that the way I carry myself, both inside and outside the boardroom, reflects Christ and the principles of my faith.

When I collaborate with people who don't share my Christian beliefs, my approach is rooted in staying true to my faith while remaining respectful of theirs. I believe it's important to be vocal about my relationship with God and my belief in Jesus Christ, but not in a way that feels pushy. The Bible calls us to stand boldly in our faith, and I carry that with me when I step into any room.

When I'm in spaces with nonbelievers, I see it as an opportunity, a moment where God may have placed me to spark curiosity or to allow others to feel His presence through me. I think about Jesus and how He interacted with others. He sat with those who were outcasts and skeptics, not to condemn them but to let His presence be felt. I strive to embody that same example, trusting that the light of God shines through me. Sometimes people can sense something different about you, even if they can't pinpoint exactly what it is. I believe that's God's presence, His light, making itself known.

In considering partnerships, again, I pray for discernment. I ask if these individuals, regardless of their beliefs, align with the vision God has placed in my heart. Will this collaboration help me achieve my goals while also offering them an experience of Christ through my actions? As Christians, we're not called to avoid those who believe differently. We're called to lead by example and show God's love by the way we show up.

———

God has blessed us all with unique purposes and talents. It's up to us to dig deep and figure out what those unique gifts are and share them with the world. And when it comes to the things we aren't good at, well, that's a great opportunity to turn to our community.

As much as we want to believe we can control every outcome, the truth is, we are all limited by our human understanding. But when you surrender to God's will and listen to His guidance above everyone else, including yourself, you can trust He

God has blessed us all with unique purposes and talents.

will guide you to relationships that will elevate you in ways you could never have imagined. Collaboration, for me, has always been grounded in that surrender—knowing that God will place the right people in my path at the right time.

There have been countless moments when I've seen God's hand at work through collaboration. One of my favorite partnerships was with Melissa Butler, the founder and CEO of The Lip Bar. Together, we created a lip and hair bundle that featured two of my favorite Mielle products alongside a custom Mielle pink lip color. What made this collaboration so special was that we developed our own unique Pantone shade—Mielle Pink—which The Lip Bar used to create a stunning lip stain. We launched this bundle online and in Target, and it performed exceptionally well. It wasn't just about the sales; it was about two Black women entrepreneurs coming together to create something meaningful for our customers.

Another memorable collaboration was with Actively Black, a brand founded by an inspiring couple. We connected through the New Voices Foundation and quickly realized how aligned we were. Our collaboration resulted in an activewear line featuring our signature Mielle Pantone color and a sleek black design for men. Again, it wasn't just about clothing—it was about creating something meaningful for both of our audiences while uplifting each other's brands.

For me, successful collaborations are rooted in reciprocity. It's not about matching followers or status but about creating value for one another. I seek out like-minded, aligned individuals who believe in the power of mutual support. Whether it's Melissa, Actively Black, or others, these partnerships allow me to not only grow my business but also give back and support other Black entrepreneurs. Together, we're stronger and more impactful when we can amplify our *collective* success.

From working with influencers to forming strategic partnerships with larger companies, every collaboration has been a stepping stone that led us closer to our goals. And even in the collaborations that didn't work out, there was always a lesson to be learned. Every experience brings growth.

I suppose I can start with Melvin. I've written a little already about how we met and the shared values and goals that led to our growing together as husband and wife. But when I look at my relationship with Melvin as a business partner, I know without a shadow of doubt that God placed us together for a reason that goes beyond just marriage. There is a purpose in our partnership, a reason why we complement each other so well. God blessed each of us with unique gifts because, again, He's clear that we were not meant to do everything on our own. Melvin and I are a great example of how people with complementary gifts and strengths can fulfill a greater purpose. There have been so many times on this journey when either Melvin or I have had to say, "I'm going to take my ego and pride out of this thing and let my partner flow in their gifts because, at the end of the day, when they win, I'm winning."

If your business partner does not have that kind of mindset, it can put a wrench in the dream. One of the best ways to navigate a healthy partnership is to know your gifts, know what you're good at, and be willing to stay in that lane for the greater good of the family and/or organization. It is much more ideal to have a partner whose skill sets complement yours. I'm strong in areas where Melvin may not be, and he excels in areas that would frustrate me to no end. It's as if God knew exactly what we both needed to build what we have.

Very early on in our business, Melvin and I identified that we had very different capacities. Our personal and business relationship could have ended in disaster if we didn't recognize how each of our skill sets complemented the other's. For instance, Melvin's background in logistics—having worked previously for major shipping companies like UPS—was incredibly useful in the management of our business's back end. His operating in the area where he was most talented—and me allowing him to do so—meant that I could focus on the areas in which I was gifted. My creative vision and marketing savvy were able to be utilized on product creation and social media engagement. Instead of one of us fighting to do it all, we embraced the areas in which we were gifted and allowed that to benefit the business.

———

No one person can be an expert in everything, and that's okay. The key is to find people whose skills and abilities align with the vision you're working toward. Not doing this, not being willing to partner with someone or collaborate, will set you and your business up for failure. Sure, as a leader, you can learn any skill you want. But remember, if you are trying to master a skill you're really not good at—or that you don't love—ask yourself if it will take too much time, effort, and energy away from being your best in your business or family. When you try to grow or accelerate beyond the pace God has set for you, things are probably not going to turn out well for you and, ultimately, you will not be the best partner or collaborator you can be.

I'm not a finance guru. I know this. I'm not the one to put the balance sheet or profit and loss statements together. I did a lot of those things in the beginning as a small business, but I often stressed trying to figure it all out. And you know what? I realized the time I spent stressing could have been better spent helping to grow the brand—because that's where my strength lay. Just because you're the CEO or the founder of your brand doesn't mean you're supposed to do everything. Your job is to master the parts you're good at, know enough about other aspects of the business so people can't get over on you, and then build a team of experts that can help sow into your vision.

I refuse to believe it is God's intention for us to struggle with no resolution. Yes, He tells us in Scripture that we will go through trials and tribulations, but He also says to take heart because He has overcome the world (John 16:33). We will go through things, but God does not intend for us to stay in those things. To be filled with the Holy Spirit means that we have access to all the ways He would want us to respond in any given situation. God didn't create us and send His Son to restore us so that we would live in a state of perpetual frustration. That's not the will of God for us. Listen, if God wanted me to be a mathematician, then He would've given me that gift. But He did not. And I'm okay with that. But that doesn't mean I can't run a business. It doesn't mean that you can't either. What it does mean is that you need to look around your community and find the person who is good at math and see if there is an opportunity for what I'll call a gift exchange. Surround yourself with people who know how to dream, and from within that community you'll find your partners.

And once again, this is where faith comes in. I believe that God intentionally places people in our path who are meant to help us achieve our purpose. Whether it's a business partner, an employee, or even a mentor, each person is part of the bigger plan.

However, if Melvin and I relied on just our complementary gifts alone, I'm not sure we would have survived all the things we've gone through. We're human. And as humans are wont to do, we could have easily allowed our egos or our limited understanding of what God was doing to get in the way of our growth. That's why it's important to have our faith grounding us. No matter how well our gifts and talents *should* work together, they only do because God is at the center. They are housed in the greater understanding that we are doing what God has called us to do. This singular fact allows me to trust my partner's judgment even when I don't fully understand it.

Trusting any partner in business or life doesn't mean blindly agreeing with them but rather believing that God brought them into your life for a reason. That kind of mindset will give you the strength to take a step back when you need to, trusting that another person's decisions are guided by the same divine purpose that guides you. You don't always have to agree on everything, but you do have to trust that God's hand is at work, even in moments of disagreement. Sometimes you may have to trust someone else more than you trust yourself. In that way, allowing a partner with a stronger gift or point of view on a topic to take over that part of your business requires humility. That's the first lesson of collaboration: Be willing to humble yourself in the face of the expertise and gifts of those you are partnering with.

There's no room for ego in a collaboration that's rooted in God's purpose. Throw that competitive spirit out the door when you are collaborating with someone. There is no competition because you both should be aligned. You should have the same goals and vision: to win. If you are letting your ego lead and competing for the spotlight, then that rivalry—even if unstated and unacknowledged—will overshadow the ultimate goal.

That's one of the things I admire most about Melvin. He has never tried to take the spotlight or outshine me, even when I'm the one being recognized publicly. It takes a strong person—a man, in particular—to be comfortable in the background, supporting someone else's success without feeling threatened or envious. Unfortunately, there are many men who are intimidated by women who are in the spotlight. They express concerns with their wives having to interact and talk with different people, including men. When I go to trade shows, it's not just women coming up to me. It's men who want to speak to me and take pictures. So it takes a very strong man to say, "I'm going to just sit back in the cut and let my wife shine." And do so without any jealousy.

I've watched so many partnerships fail because of ego—whether in marriage or business. People become so consumed with getting credit or being in the spotlight that they forget the bigger picture. But again, that's where faith comes in. When you truly believe that God has a plan for both of you, it becomes easier to let go of that need for recognition. Melvin understands that the success of our business is a reflection of both of our efforts, even if I'm the one in the limelight.

Ego—the part of us that is consumed with our own self-importance—is the single most pervasive barrier in partnerships. It keeps us from fully realizing the blessings that come with collaboration. When you set your ego aside, you allow God to work in ways that are far beyond what you could ever achieve on your own. In fact, collaboration requires a willingness to step back. The ability to say, "I don't have to do this all myself. I don't need all the credit. I trust that God will elevate us together." That's a lesson I've had to learn repeatedly, and it's one I see echoed in Scripture over and over again. God doesn't reward selfish ambition. He blesses those who work together in humility and faith.

———

Another important aspect of collaboration is communication, and for me, that, too, is rooted in faith. Communication is not just about talking; it's about understanding the heart of the person you're working with. Listen, some conflict can be resolved by just having a conversation. Everyone is entitled to their feelings. I don't have to agree with every decision my partners make, but holding frustration in never helps. It will only fester and cause resentment unless I talk with the person. And the point of talking is not just so I can relieve myself of my frustration but so I can also listen. By listening, I'm able to hear the other person's reasoning. I still might not agree, but I will at least learn more about that person's perspective and where they are coming from.

Communication is not just about talking; it's about understanding the heart of the person you're working with.

Melvin and I have had many disagreements about business decisions, often revolving around the people who work in our organization. Do we hire that person? Do we fire this one? We've also questioned whether to pivot the brand into a different category. Do we move into skincare or not? Those disagreements, however, never turn into lasting conflicts because we always come back to one thing: our shared purpose. When we talk things out, we realize it's not about who is right or wrong but about finding common ground or a compromise that serves the greater good of our business and our family. That kind of communication is only possible when we both have the same vision and the same God guiding that vision.

Compromise is not an easy thing to do, but when God is at the center, it becomes easier to think or say, "Okay. I'm going to lose this battle because it makes more sense and will lead to greater things for the business or my family." You might not be willing to compromise if it's just you and this other person and all your big feelings about an issue. But if God is in the mix and you have committed to trusting Him, then you are more willing to compromise, knowing that, in the end, it's a win for the greater vision. No matter how much we may argue or how many meetings it takes, I want a partner with whom I can come back to common ground and ask, "Is the fight really worth it?" Nine times out of ten, it isn't.

The same is true when it comes to how we resolve conflict. In any partnership, moments of tension or disagreement are inevitable. But when you're both grounded in shared values, it becomes easier to approach those conflicts with a spirit of understanding and grace. I've learned to pray through disagreements, asking God to reveal the right path, even when my emotions are clouding my judgment. Sometimes that means admitting when I'm wrong, and other times it means trusting my partner's instincts over my own. Your willingness to be vulnerable is often the key to collaborating in any meaningful way. Vulnerability can cut through any battle of wills that shows up. It can transform a struggle for control into something beautiful—a shared journey toward a common goal.

Collaboration also teaches us patience. Not every partnership will yield immediate results, and sometimes it takes time for the fruits of your labor to show. It's not easy, but you'll soon learn to trust in the timing of things and not rush the process because you know God is working everything out in His timing. I've had to remind myself of this many times, especially when things weren't moving as quickly as I wanted them to. God's timing is perfect, even when it doesn't align with my expectations.

———

In life, particularly as a business owner, you need discernment when choosing partners. Not everyone who pitches you an idea or who comes to you wanting to collaborate has your best interests at heart. There have been times when I've been blindsided by people who I thought were trustworthy, only to find out they were looking out for themselves. That's why it's important to seek God's guidance when forming partnerships. As I've said, I've learned to pray for discernment, asking God to reveal people's true intentions. And every time I've ignored that gut feeling, that still small voice warning me about someone, it's led to trouble.

When trying to figure out whether to partner with someone or some entity, pay attention to those red flags. I like to examine a person's character. How do they treat people from whom they can't benefit? I've been in situations where a person I was considering collaborating with, someone who was perfectly fine toward me, treated someone else terribly. To the extent I had to wonder, *This person is so mean and nasty, but yet they're nice to me. Why is that?* The answer was usually because that's who they are. They were nice to me because they felt like they could get something from our relationship, yet they treated everyone else like trash. That's a huge red flag every time. Have you witnessed this yourself? One of the first things I do when selecting a business partner is look at how that person conducts themselves when no one is watching.

There was one woman we partnered with who was very nice—to us. Whenever we met, she was professional and cordial, and overall, there was no reason for us to believe our collaboration would be a problem. Yet, whenever we'd send her out to meet with various vendors or contractors, some kind of major conflict would arise. It didn't happen just once or twice. It happened nearly every single time. When we'd ask her about it, she'd always play the victim and say it was not her fault. She kept pointing the finger at the vendors and claiming that they were the problem, but I didn't buy that. If there are ten people from ten different walks of life, and you have a major blowup with all ten, there's only one common denominator. You! So now I make sure I set up situations where I can observe potential partners outside of the business they conduct with me. Because the last thing I want in my business ecosystem is someone who is pretending to be a partner when they are really a predator.

In that same vein, I also ask, "Is this person honest?" I've had partnerships with people who didn't tell the truth. If you really pay attention to a person's conversations, you can often tell when they're lying. Their stories will switch up and nothing's ever the same. Dishonest people, in my experience, also gossip more than most. I pay attention to whether the person is always bad-mouthing other people. That's a good indication they don't have a moral compass and can't be trusted. For instance, I've had people come to me to pitch a collaboration opportunity, but while doing so they spend time bad-mouthing the previous company they worked for. Red flag! I don't want them working for me either, especially since they've now shown me that they come with drama.

Being scammed is the worst. It hurts when you've been taken advantage of by people who seemed genuine but were really just looking for a way to benefit themselves. But even in those painful experiences, I've seen God's hand at work. Remember how messed up our books had been? When we initially began our search for a CFO, we were introduced to an accountant management company who said they could reorganize and restructure our books.

When they came out to meet with us, I should have known that they weren't going to be good partners. They were fast-talkers. You know the kind? Salesy people who talk in circles and don't let you get a word in edgewise. I'm not the loudest person in the room, but when I do speak, what I have to say is very important. I don't feel the need to overtalk to get my point across, and I certainly don't have to be loud to make my presence known. That was clearly not how this company rolled. I've heard that people who speak faster are perceived as being smarter, and that must be right since we were mostly convinced. But my gut was sending alarms, telling me that something was not right with these people, and much of what they were saying didn't feel accurate. I stayed up many nights googling, trying to figure out if what they were asking and doing was standard in the industry. Our need was so great that I ended up ignoring my intuition and signing on with them to do our books.

"We will need to be a signer on your bank accounts," they said.

Wait, what? This was a huge red flag. We didn't know much, but we knew that wasn't going to work.

"No, you're not going to be a signer on our account."

Everything shifted when we told them no. They tried to use all kinds of fear tactics when explaining what might happen if we didn't allow them to be a signer. It really started to feel awkward because they kept pressing. It was strange.

The next fear tactic they used was related to our taxes.

"Your accountant screwed up everything. You guys are going to have this big tax bill."

Of course. That's why we hired you.

But then they turned the fire up: "You can go to jail for this."

Again, it was all a manipulation tactic. They were pretending to be doing their job in protecting us, but really they just wanted to be signers on our account for their own nefarious reasons. That's the thing with most scammers. They'll do just enough to prove they are what they portray themselves to be, just enough to get you to trust them. But when you don't succumb to all their machinations, they will often get angry or try to tear you down.

Thankfully, we shared what we were experiencing with other trusted businesses, and they began to educate us. We could have been too embarrassed to say anything. To ask questions. But we weren't and that worked in our favor. Don't be afraid to share what you're going through with people who have been in your shoes and can give you sound advice. We learned that so much of what these people were telling us was not true. They didn't need to be signers on our account. The tax situation wasn't as dire as they were making it out to be. Eventually, we got to the point where we sent them a letter terminating their services. Unfortunately, when we finally got our books back, they were completely destroyed.

It's important to note that in business and in everyday life, sometimes it's not a matter of a person or entity being an intentional scammer. Sometimes they are just incompetent and don't realize it. They have talked themselves into believing they are the greatest (insert title here) on earth. But when it comes down to fulfilling what they promise, it's easy to determine that they have very limited capacity or simply are not good at what they do—but they've been "successful" because they've been able to put forth a facade to make people think they're better than they are. Nevertheless, there are definitely vultures out there looking for young entrepreneurs or people with very little experience and desperate for collaboration to prey on. Be smart and resourceful enough to ask questions. Listen to the Holy Spirit. Don't be too desperate to ask, "Are these the right people for us? Is this the partner God is sending?" At the end of the day, know that when people let you down, God never does. He has a way of redirecting your path, even when it feels like everything is falling apart.

> God has a way of redirecting your path, even when it feels like everything is falling apart.

All of our not-so-great experiences taught me so much about what to look for in a partner. They taught me what I don't want, but they also revealed to me the qualities of a great collaborator. We've had so many people on our team who were willing to roll up their sleeves, get their hands dirty, and grind it out with us in this business. They were willing to grow. We knew they were in our corner, and I'm so grateful for them. But not every partnership is meant to last. Some collaborations will be temporary, and that's okay. People change—as will your business—so it's good to be mindful of when you and a partner need to go separate ways. In any collaboration, business or otherwise, begin on a firm foundation, and the likelihood that success will find you is greater—no matter the duration of the partnership.

With the exception of maybe your life partner, there will be people who will come in and out of your life. They might even feel like family, and you will grieve their loss as such. We had employees and collaborators who were amazing in the early stages, but as we expanded, their skills and mindsets weren't aligned with where we were headed. That's not to say they didn't contribute to our success—they did—but at a certain point, you will likely recognize when it's time to move on.

There were times when I felt devastated by the loss of certain partnership opportunities, particularly when I had invested so much time and energy into them. But I now see that God was pruning those relationships for a reason. Not everyone who starts the journey with you is meant to finish it with you. Letting go of those relationships, even when it hurts, is another sign that you are listening to God's direction and guidance and trusting that He has something better in store for you, even when you can't see it in the moment.

Collaboration, when done right, can be a reflection of God's grace. The trust it requires allows you to approach every partnership with an open heart, knowing that even if things don't work out the way you hoped, God is still in control. Whether it's collaborating with your spouse or a family member, partnering with other businesses, or working with your employees, try to approach each relationship with the belief that God is guiding your steps. He

Not everyone who starts the journey with you is meant to finish it with you.

is always working behind the scenes, placing the right people in your life and removing the ones who are no longer meant to be on your journey.

In fact, God uses collaboration to elevate us. Being open to partnerships means you are also open to allowing God to work through others to help you grow. Sometimes that growth comes in the form of learning hard lessons—about trust, about humility, about forgiveness. We are still stronger together than we are alone. By working with the right people at the right time, we allow God's purpose to be fulfilled in ways we couldn't achieve on our own.

QUESTIONS FOR REFLECTION

- Think about a successful business or organizational collaboration you've experienced. What qualities did your partner bring to the table that complemented your own strengths? How did this contribute to the overall success of the project?
- Reflect on a time when your intuition or gut guided you in a relationship, either positively or negatively. How did trusting—or ignoring—your intuition affect the outcome?

11

Selling Up, Not Out

Guiding Principle:
Validation is for parking and nothing more.

CONSIDERING WHAT I'D LEARNED ABOUT COLLABORA-
tion, our decision to sell Mielle Organics to Procter & Gamble while
retaining operational roles was one of the biggest decisions we ever made
and the biggest deal we've ever done. It required having a grasp of the
delicate balance between scaling a business and maintaining that business's core values and authenticity. However, not everyone understood
or embraced our decision. On any given day after the announcement,
we were called "sellouts" who betrayed the Black community in favor of
money.

That was so incredibly far from the truth.

I cannot emphasize enough the challenges we were facing in 2018
when Mielle was $2 million in debt. Every day was a battle to keep our
heads above water. We'd poured everything into this business—our time,
money, and energy. And when you're in that deep, you feel like you can't
afford to fail. But we kept pushing and kept fighting. And during that
time, we began to consider private equity firms, which would invest in

our privately owned company in exchange for an interest stake in the business. The partnership with Richelieu Dennis and New Voices Fund—more on that later—came just as we were beginning to find our footing again. That investment wasn't just a financial boost; it was a lifeline. It was evidence that someone else believed in the potential of Mielle as much as we did. We took that investment and turned it into something unheard of and unseen since.

When the COVID-19 pandemic hit, the world was thrown into unexpected grief and chaos like I'd never seen in my lifetime. Industries faltered. Businesses that had been around for decades closed up shop. The landscape of beauty changed during the pandemic because people still had to show up for work. But now work was on Zoom. Women were trying to figure out how to manage their hair and look presentable when they had to go on camera. At first, it seemed like no big deal. At most, maybe it was an inconvenience for those who were used to seeing their time at the salon as a way to connect with other women and a form of self-care. But soon, I saw something subtle and beautiful unfolding. Black women were at home and discovering, some for the first time, the power and beauty of their natural hair textures. Out of necessity, they were learning to love and care for their hair in ways they maybe hadn't before. And it wasn't just them. I remember cutting off four inches of my own hair during lockdown. There I was, in my bathroom, staring at the mirror, scissors in hand, thinking about all the roads my hair had traveled on this journey with me. It was freeing. Cathartic, even. And as I let those damaged ends fall, I realized that I was shedding more than hair. I was shedding doubt, fear, and maybe a little boredom.

Very similar to the early 1970s and the late 1990s, the Black hair community was once again embracing the diversity and beauty of our hair. Mostly because we finally had the time to play in it. Twist outs. Locs. Silk presses. Braids. It was all on the table. It just made sense to me to turn these observations into useful intel for my business. As women were exploring hairstyles, they were also trying new products. And Mielle was right there alongside them, providing what they needed. I'd like to think that it was more than just hair care, though. It was about self-acceptance.

As a result of being able to tap into this need during an otherwise bleak period, our business boomed. Other companies and industries were barely holding on, but we were growing faster than ever, nearly quadrupling our sales from the previous year. But then another shift happened, one that would make us take a hard look at who we were and what we stood for.

The summer of 2020 arrived, and with it, the murder of George Floyd. As the video of a Minneapolis police officer kneeling on George's neck while he cried out for his mother made its rounds on social media, the world—still in the throes of a pandemic—seemed to stop. We were forced to collectively grieve that loss as well as reckon with what it meant for Black and Brown people to be overwhelmingly the targets of excessive force and violence by police. The streets were filled with protests and voices crying out for justice, for change. And suddenly, there was a surge of support for Black-owned businesses. People were looking for ways to stand in solidarity, and one of those ways was by buying from companies like ours. It was a bittersweet moment. On the one hand, we were seeing unprecedented support. On the other, that support was a constant reminder of the pain and struggle our community faces every day.

I remember the pressure I felt to speak out. There were so many who wanted me to show up in a very visible way. Understandably, they wanted to know where I stood. They expected a post, a statement, something they could share and say, "See, Mielle is with us!" But I chose a slightly different, yet still public, path. Instead of making static posts on social media, I went live on Mielle's platforms to pray. I prayed for our community, for peace, and for justice. I prayed for change in our systems and in the hearts of those who wrongly feel empowered by their ability to oppress others. I felt like prayer was way more impactful than a social media post, but I soon learned that this wasn't the response people were looking for.

I was criticized terribly. Many in my own community said I wasn't showing enough support and that I was being insensitive by not post-ing videos of the violent injustices and the subsequent protests. Everyone wanted me to respond in a way that aligned with their expectations, which was impossible because everyone's idea of "enough support" was differ-ent. I couldn't have made everyone happy even if I tried. But I knew that prayer was the most powerful tool I had. I wasn't interested in performa-tive activism. Posting black boxes and sharing traumatic video footage on social media didn't feel productive. It certainly brought awareness, which is good. Everyone copes with things differently. But to me, it also brought a lot of sadness. I didn't want my page to be a site of sadness and pain. I wanted to create space for real healing.

The backlash was tough, though. There was a big social media trolling incident where people started calling me out, saying I didn't support the Black Lives Matter movement. In that moment, I felt like my own people were coming against me. They were attacking me for what I thought was the best way to handle the situation. My pastor had always told me that "with prosperity comes persecution," but this was a lot.

It hurt to see people questioning my commitment to the cause, espe-cially when I felt so deeply connected to it. The world was in such a crazy state, though. In one breath, people wanted to support each other, but in the next, if you weren't supporting in the way this group or that group thought you should, or if you weren't following what the crowd was doing, then you'd be treated as an outcast. I had to remind myself that authen-ticity often comes with a price. I stood by my approach because I knew I was doing what felt right to me.

It's not always easy, but I believe that each of us has to walk our own path. For me, that path includes prayer and faith. I had to trust that my actions, even if misunderstood, were contributing to the greater good. I also had to trust that it would not hurt the business we were building. So in this season, there was both positive and negative noise in the media about Mielle. People were rooting for us because we were Black-owned, but at the same time, they were tearing me down.

While I would have preferred to avoid the bad publicity, it was still publicity. And the company continued to grow. People became curious about me and Mielle, and once they saw my character and understood what we were trying to do, they eventually started supporting us. That's a huge lesson: No matter what people say about you, if you stay true to yourself, your character will override what others are saying. And that's exactly what happened.

As 2021 approached, Mielle was still growing at a rate we hadn't anticipated. It was at this point we knew that if we wanted to continue on this trajectory, we would need help. This is when Berkshire Partners entered the picture, and their investment set us up for the bigger deal with P&G.

Working with Richelieu (Rich) and New Voices allowed us to get the business into a healthy, profitable state. Once we reached that point, the quadruple growth we were experiencing meant we were finally not operating in the negative. This turned everything around. More private equity firms were now chomping at the bit to be a part of Mielle because we were a healthy company. Our numbers were unheard of, especially for being in business for only six years. Down the road, if we stayed the course, this would make us extremely attractive to potential buyers.

One rule of thumb I learned from my CFO is this: The best time to raise money for your business is when you don't need it, because then you have all the leverage. When you're not begging for money, you're in a position to ask them, "How can you partner with us to help us get to the next level?" To become the global brand we intended to be, we wanted to eventually have a successful exit. That was always the goal—but we knew the prerequisites to achieving that.

We could have gone straight to a strategic partner like P&G and said, "Hey, buy us now." But we knew the value of our company, and we knew we could reach a level of value that we'd be comfortable with when the time came for acquisition. If we had made the deal with Rich and then sought acquisition, we might not have been valued as highly because, at that time, we were still working on growing revenue. We recognized that with the momentum we had, we could grow our revenue even more over the next couple of years, which would lead to our business being worth more when a strategic partner approached us.

To achieve this, partnering with another private equity firm was the way to go. They could bring more resources, support, and infrastructure, helping us hire C-suite executives who could scale the business. I think a lot of people don't realize that as a founder, you can only grow your company to a certain point, but then the company can start growing faster than your expertise. That's when that humility I talked about earlier is essential. You have to be able to say, "It's growing faster than I can keep up." At that point, you bring in experts who've been down this road before and can leverage their knowledge, resources, and connections to help you scale to a new level.

So I told Melvin I thought we should raise money. "Really?" he replied. "Yes, because the best time to raise money is when you don't need it. We have leverage right now; we are being watched—let's go for it. Let's see what we're valued at, and if it's lucrative, let's take a first bite at the apple."

And that's what we did.

Also, this was going to be a win for us as a family. When you are a profitable company, and you do a deal with a private equity firm when your company is healthy, the money they invest does not go to your balance sheet. It goes to the founders.

When we sat down to negotiate with Berkshire, we had already met with over sixty different private equity companies. Not because we needed to, like before, but because the brand was so enticing that everyone was asking to meet with us. That was such a great feeling. Coming from where we started, digging ourselves out of a hole, to now having everyone wanting to talk to us. People were even begging our bankers for a chance to speak with us. It was mind-blowing.

I recognize that some of this interest was influenced by what was going on in the world. Frankly, in light of George Floyd's death and the ongoing fight against racial injustice and police brutality, white people were feeling sorry for Black people. It's unfortunate that it took something so tragic for some to develop the empathy and compassion they should have always had. So yes, many of these predominately white-owned companies were trying to figure out how to provide opportunities to Black businesses. Hence all the interest. But even so, they weren't going to just give money away. Not at the level we were at. We checked all the boxes *and* were a great investment.

———

Opportunities often come when you least expect them, and the key to success is being ready when they do. I've seen firsthand how preparation can set you apart. As the saying goes, "Be ready so you don't have to get ready." It's about staying prepared, building a strong foundation, and ensuring your business—or whatever you're pursuing—can stand on its own. When the opportunity comes, there's no time to scramble. Your preparation speaks for you, and that's what opens doors. Whether it's in business or life, put in the work now so you're ready for what's next.

I'm so glad we met with those sixty companies, though. Not because I enjoyed it—the introvert in me dreaded all those conversations and presentations. But what I loved was that it was normalizing these conversations for those companies. They were sitting down with Black owners who had built a successful company from the ground up, faced challenges, and come out stronger on the other side. This was foreign to many of them. They didn't believe companies like ours could exist. But there we were, showing them what was possible and hopefully making it easier for them to sit down with the next Black-owned business.

After narrowing those sixty private equity firms down to three, we chose Berkshire, who stood out the most. They had the most value, and they also donated a million dollars to our foundation. That offer set the stage for the opportunity that would come next.

Berkshire saw what we were building and wanted to be a part of it.

Partnering with them was a significant step, finalizing this amazing deal in March 2021. While we brought them on as private equity investors, we retained our majority ownership, which was crucial for us at that time and a big deal. I was the first African American woman in the beauty space to partner with a private equity firm while still maintaining majority ownership. Most of the time, such firms want to own a majority share of the company they're investing millions into. Not doing so is a huge risk, since a founder could just as easily cash the check and run off to Greece to live on a yacht or something. But Berkshire trusted that Melvin and I were good, trustworthy people. They felt our passion and saw our work ethic. From our perspective, we wanted to grow, but on our own terms.

Even with the support of Berkshire, I knew some people in the Black community worried that we would have to surrender what made Mielle great. That, with the encouragement of this firm, we'd become so focused on growing that we'd leave behind the consumers who rocked with us from the beginning. Yes, there are horror stories of private equity companies coming in and taking over in this way, which is why we maintained that majority ownership.

There's a fear in our community that growth means compromise, that scaling up means selling out. It's a valid fear. Again, born from a long history of seeing Black-owned businesses struggle to maintain their authenticity as they expand. Also, misconceptions exist in the Black community because, frankly, there haven't been enough Black brands that have successfully scaled. The masses don't really understand what it takes to do that. And of course, people fear what they don't understand. When you've only seen two other brands before Mielle do a deal of this size, and you know the challenges they faced, it's easy to assume the same will happen to Mielle. But that's not always the case. Studying other businesses that did it the wrong way, we learned how to structure better deals, and we hope businesses that come after us will learn from our experience.

I think some of the attachments Black people have to our businesses have to do with the language we use. There were so many people who said

Mielle had to stay Black-owned. They didn't care that we were growing and needed help to grow more. They were just hung up on that language: Black-owned, not Black-founded, as we identify ourselves today. Yes, there is a special kind of cultural power and pride in being Black-owned and smaller. Local community businesses are absolutely necessary, and one of the ways those businesses can stay around is through the efforts of larger companies like Mielle that position themselves to gain the resources to pour back into those communities. And frankly, what if your business wasn't worth much, or anything at all? If you could partner with someone to grow your business while maintaining majority control, then you could do more for yourself, your family, and your community. Would you rather own 100 percent of nothing or 51 percent of a thriving, financially successful business? It was never about losing what makes Mielle special but about amplifying it. By expanding our reach and resources, we've been able to serve our people more.

Greatness is still possible without having to compromise. Yes, some of that will be contingent on your discernment, your ability to choose partners and opportunities that give you the freedom to maintain your ideals. But you don't have to lose your values or your vision to grow. Sometimes it's about shifting your perspective, redefining success, and taking bold steps to ensure your business reaches its full potential. Don't be afraid to seek greatness—it's worth it.

I didn't even see the path to selling until I was exposed to it, which is exactly why exposure is such a gift. When Rich sold Shea Moisture to Unilever, it was my first time seeing what was possible. My eyes lit up. I even cut out an article with the headline and put it on my vision board, gluing a picture of Melvin and me over the image of Rich and his

Greatness is still possible without having to compromise.

mom. It was my way of visualizing what could be. That moment lit a fire in me that burned until we were sitting at our own table, signing our deal. That fire still burns to this day. I've always understood the fear, but I also know that in order to reach more people, we had to think bigger. We had to envision the company bigger. We weren't just building a business; we were building a movement.

Many people don't understand how deals are negotiated. Some brands may have more leverage or power when they make deals. Others don't. Unless you're part of the negotiations, you don't know the circumstances behind an acquisition. This is the primary reason why I chose to be as transparent as possible, letting our people know up front what to expect—what would likely happen and what wasn't going to change—all while standing firm on the trustworthy brand we built. And I must say, since we were acquired in 2023, the brand has stayed true. Contrary to what some people believe, the formulas haven't changed. We are still very much Black-owned in spirit. When we go to our events, we still swag surf. Again, when it comes to our principles, commitment to excellence, and keeping our customers as our main focus, nothing has changed. The authenticity of the brand is still there. And when people encounter me, they're still going to see "CEO" in my bio.

Following the Berkshire deal, we finally got the leverage we needed to play with the big dogs. Interest had come from Procter & Gamble in the summer of 2022. We didn't know they had been watching us for years. We were later told that they had, for a while, been trying to assess whether our brand would sustain. We were growing and looked great, but how long would we be around? So when the opportunity finally presented itself, they were eager to acquire us. There were other companies interested in doing a deal, so it wasn't a cut-and-dried process. We didn't decide to go with P&G until December of that year.

In the thick of negotiations—having late-night Zoom calls and working to get the contracts signed—Melvin and I asked for an emergency meeting with our pastor at 10 p.m. When we arrived, we explained what was happening and what we were about to do. At the time, we were torn between great deals from two amazing companies, P&G and another. "We need prayer," we said. "We need guidance." After praying with us, our pastor, who didn't know who P&G was at the time (we explained they probably make his toothpaste), said, "There's something about this P&G that keeps jumping out in my spirit." It was confirmation. I'd been feeling the same way and didn't really know why. We closed the deal in January 2023.

People who had been side-eyeing us because of the Berkshire private equity deal didn't like that we were now aligned with such a large corporation, especially a predominately white one. A certain subset of our community now viewed Mielle as just another brand that sold out, one that diluted its soul to appeal to a broader audience.

But here's what I held on to: I *knew* I'd heard from God on the matter. I had prayed about this impossible-at-the-time hope of partnering with a conglomerate like P&G long before it became a reality. Many months before P&G even reached out to us, I had written the following in my journal:

Mielle will be acquired by P&G.

I had forgotten all about that entry until after we closed the deal and I came across it randomly one day. But God hadn't forgotten. That entry would become a guiding light for me. A reminder and affirmation that God's hand was in this. It was His nod of "well done," revealing that this was the path we were meant to take. This would not only mean success for Mielle but, as I've said, ultimately allow us to serve our community *more* and not less. And in a much more expansive way. What many of these skeptics and armchair critics didn't know or see was the depth of our commitment to Mielle. They didn't see the hours we spent negotiating that deal, the tough conversations we had to ensure our mission would remain intact. When we began discussions with P&G, they made it clear that they understood our mission and would honor it. They knew we weren't just another beauty brand. They saw the impact we were having on our community, and they wanted to support that. And what sealed the deal despite us having multiple offers on the table was when P&G offered to pledge $10 million to support our initiatives in Black communities. That wasn't something we asked for; it was something they offered. And that's when I knew we had found the right partner. They were choosing to invest in more than just our products; they were investing in our values, in the legacy we were building.

In spite of all the positivity from this deal, the ensuing backlash came swiftly and with great intensity. I still tried to hold on to the part of me that understood why this was happening. I knew that we weren't just trying to get a big check and walk away. We were still trying to build something that would stand the test of time. But I also felt like the last thing our community should want is to tear down brands that choose to scale, to the point where strategic companies are afraid to acquire Black brands at all. Because then what? Do we just stop growing?

If I were an investor like P&G, I might be scared to invest in Black businesses nowadays because it would seem like no matter how great the product is, how positive and impactful the organization and its leaders are, there's a chance that its audience will turn its back on it once acquired. This was why, when Rich went through the same kind of backlash for selling Shea Moisture to Unilever, I not only reached out with our support but also sat on a panel defending him. Apparently, I was the only owner to do this. And when it was our turn, we experienced a similar vacuum. Only one brand reached out to us with support. Thankfully, I didn't have any expectations that we would be treated differently. Sometimes it felt like other brands were waiting for something negative to happen.

When Berkshire and P&G both asked about how the Black community would react to their partnerships with us, I quickly responded, "Do you ask other brands that question?" And they said no. Private equity and venture capital firms are always going to be hyperconscious of how the Black community will feel about a potential buy. It gives them pause when there's always the kind of uproar we experienced, and that can mess up the growth potential and possibilities for Black businesses overall. If we keep pushing the "sellout" narrative, companies will take their money elsewhere, and one more path to generational wealth will close to us. This is why we were very careful about how we structured our deal with P&G. I stayed on as CEO and Melvin as COO of the company. We maintained the formulas of the products. With P&G's support, we were able to fund projects like Mielle Cares, initiatives that provide resources and opportunities to Black communities. We became the first Black-founded hair care brand associated with the Olympics and the WNBA. The Olympics has never had a textured hair care brand as a sponsor, but now they have a Black brand because these Black athletes need to be serviced too.

These weren't just wins for us. We see them as victories for our entire community. They show that we can serve our community while reaching for new heights. We made it clear from the beginning that this wasn't just about us. This was about creating a platform that would inspire other Black businesses to dream bigger.

———

If I'm honest, one of the hardest parts of this journey has been staying true to my faith in the face of such heartbreaking criticism. It is frustrating because I firmly believe that no one has a right to criticize what God has placed in my heart—the vision He gave me. Especially without the facts. And if you do criticize the purpose that God has given me, then you are basically criticizing Him. And I somehow don't think that's going to work out very well for you.

Yet, I've still been called every name in the book. I've had other brands use individuals to sabotage the integrity of Mielle. Most recently, there was an uproar on social media started by a few influencers alleging that Mielle products could cause hair breakage and loss. *That* was the one that both broke my heart and enraged me at the same time. This ongoing conversation about how our formulas have changed since the

P&G sale was patently false. I knew that, and anyone who even took half a second to evaluate the product labels knew that. And yet, these falsehoods ignited a whirlwind of accusation, drawing not just people who might have genuinely struggled with finding the right product for their hair but clout-chasers and hangers-on who wanted to use the controversy as an opportunity to gain more clicks and status. And then to later learn that some of these individuals possibly were motivated to do so by competing brands—well, that challenged the gangster in this girl from the South Side of Chicago in every single way. Nevertheless, I made a statement, did an interview to clear up the issue, and let my legal team handle the rest.

I could have gotten down in the dirt with those who were making these false claims. But isn't that what the Enemy wants? To drive us into the gutter so that we forget who we are and whose we are? With every accusation and negative post or article, I leaned on prayer. I had to *trust* that God was guiding us. I knew that this deal with P&G wasn't going to be understood by everyone, but I also knew that I didn't need the world's approval. I needed to be faithful to the path God had set before me.

———

While it is important to talk about, I don't mean to harp on the criticism. The truth is, we've also seen tremendous support from our community. But as usual, the squeaky wheel gets the oil, the attention. Through it all, I just wish the Black community could give our businesses the freedom to pursue *whatever* path we choose. If a business decides to stay small and serve its local community because that's its vision and purpose, then great. If someone takes the money from selling a business they built and sails off into the sunset, more power to them. Building something from scratch is hard, so I get the desire to retire and rest. Most critics haven't built anything. And if someone sells their company and uses that money to develop the community, that's wonderful. Whatever a person feels committed to and good about should be celebrated. Because that's true freedom.

In the end, our decision to sell to P&G wasn't just a business move. It was a chance to bring Mielle to a global audience and normalize Black success on a scale we hadn't yet achieved.

Friend, when the Lord tells you to move, don't hesitate. Don't wait for the validation of others. Don't even pause when the Enemy of your soul turns up the heat. Simply trust that God knows the way, and you follow where He leads. The truth is, God didn't give that vision to others. He gave it to you. The dream in your heart, the direction you're moving toward, is uniquely yours. You can't expect everyone to understand why you do what you do or the decisions you make, and that's okay. Your vision isn't for them; it's for you. You don't need anyone else's permission to follow your purpose.

When the Lord tells you to move, don't hesitate. Don't wait for the validation of others.

To remain grounded, I've had to develop tunnel vision, staying focused on God's promises even when distractions come. People's opinions often shift with the wind, but my faith doesn't. That's why it's crucial to have a strong foundation: Read God's Word, pray, and surround yourself with people who will encourage you in your walk. You need a support system that reminds you of God's truth when you're feeling down—friends who will push you to open your Bible, pray for you when you can't pray for yourself, and speak life into your dreams.

Growth doesn't mean selling out; it means amplifying your voice and reaching more people. With P&G, we are able to take Mielle to places we could only dream of before. Yes, we did the deal to elevate our brand, but more importantly, we did it to create opportunities to uplift. Sure, there will be people who will try to box you in, limiting your success to what makes sense to them. But God didn't create you to live in a box—He created you to live an exceedingly abundant life. Expanding beyond that box might cause others to criticize or hate you, but that's not your burden to bear. When you are clear about why you are doing something, don't let criticism stop you. It's just noise. Stay focused on what matters, and let the world catch up later. We didn't sell out. We scaled up. There's a difference. Ignore your naysayers. That's what we did and will continue to do.

QUESTIONS FOR REFLECTION

- Think about a time when you were met with resistance or skepticism for a decision you felt was right. How did you rely on your faith to stay committed? What role does prayer play in helping you silence the noise and trust God's plan over the need for public approval?
- As you consider scaling up or taking a leap that might draw scrutiny, how do you define success in a way that aligns with your faith and values? What would it look like to pursue growth not for validation but as a means to serve and uplift others?

12

We Can All Win

Guiding Principle:
Ignore the naysayers and haters,
but don't become one.

ABOUT THOSE NAYSAYERS.

It takes confidence to support others, to cheer for them without feeling threatened. But I've learned that confidence isn't something you're born with; it's something you build over time. I've built mine by staying true to myself and trusting that what's meant for me will come to me. But I've also met people who want what I have, not because they admire it or are inspired by it, but because they believe I don't deserve it. Those encounters are always reminders that our fight is rarely against flesh and blood but against spiritual forces. It's not always these people at work. Nine times out of ten it's these people allowing themselves to be used by something way more nefarious to thwart what God is trying to do. These naysayers tear others down to feel good about themselves. To feel successful. But it's often way bigger than them. Bigger than me. This is why I've learned to not concern myself with any naysayer. In fact, I recommend shifting your focus from the naysayers to your cheerleaders.

Confidence isn't something you're born with; it's something you build over time.

The best way for you to build a community of cheerleaders is by being open, transparent, and, most importantly, your authentic self. When you show up as your true self, the right people—the ones assigned to your journey—will be drawn to you. Those are the people you should focus on. Don't waste energy on the negative voices or naysayers, because what you focus on will grow. If you pour into the positive, your community of supporters will naturally thrive.

That doesn't mean ignoring all criticism. Some feedback, even if it's less constructive than you'd like, can help you grow and improve. But don't let it get so deep into your spirit that you begin to doubt yourself or the vision God has given you. Stay grounded in who you are, and let your authenticity be the foundation for building relationships. Focusing on your cheerleaders—those who truly believe in you and your mission— will allow you to create a supportive community that honors the path God has placed you on. Don't mind the naysayer and don't become one. The mission is always to stand in your own light and celebrate the light in others.

Throughout my journey with Mielle, I've encountered more resistance than I ever anticipated. What surprised me most wasn't the general competition in the larger beauty industry. It was the intense negativity from other Black woman–owned brands. There's a deeply rooted mentality among some that there can only be one or two uber-successful Black businesses at a time. This belief, in my opinion, is a product of both the systemic racism and sexism we've all faced.

The Black beauty business, while originally pioneered by women like Annie Turnbo Malone and Madam C. J. Walker, stayed mostly male-dominated for a long time. Think Dudley's or Johnson's products. Only in the past fifteen years or so has it become more female dominated. When I started Mielle, I was excited to enter a space where I could collaborate and grow with other Black women. I thought we would celebrate each other's successes. I thought we could push each other to greater heights. But from the beginning, I encountered competitors who believed that my success meant their downfall. They seemed to be stuck in this mindset that there wasn't enough room for all of us, that for one to rise, another must fall. It was almost as if they had convinced themselves that the industry wasn't ready for more than one success story. And so, instead of supporting each other, they set out to undermine anyone new who came in. In 2014, that new face was Mielle.

I have allies in the business, for sure, but from the start, the overwhelming response to Mielle seemed to be negative or, at best, apathetic. Granted, some of this can be attributed to us coming out of nowhere and disrupting the industry. People were likely thinking, *Where did this brand come from? We've been doing this forever, and here's this new brand coming on the scene and just taking over.* Meanwhile, we were simply doing what God called us to, making mistakes along the way but learning from them quickly.

Nevertheless, it's been disheartening to experience direct and indirect injuries from people I thought would be supportive. I've felt that tension whenever I walked into a room with other brands present. I've heard the chatter about how other Black female–led brands felt about me. I've gone into retail buying meetings and heard about how people tried to sabotage our brand or steal shelf space from us. And we can't forget how Mielle has been treated online. Many brands have blocked me on various platforms and made it clear that they don't want anything to do with my success. In the world of social media, blocking someone is a statement. It's a way of saying, "I don't want to see you, I don't want to support you, and I don't want you to exist in my space." My team would try to send me posts from these brands, and I'd have to tell them I couldn't view the content because I was blocked. It was almost amusing at times, the lengths they would go. *Almost.* It also stung a little. Always, it was a reminder that they saw me as a threat, not as someone to walk alongside.

And then there was the time a competitor went out of their way to use one of our products in a promotional video. They posted the video featuring our hair oil side by side with theirs. You could tell there was a half-hearted attempt to blur out our label, but it was clearly our packaging. The message was clear: "Here's why my product is better." But why? That's what I call dirty marketing. They didn't need to do that. In business, you don't have to play dirty to win. And most likely, that kind of thing will backfire in the long run anyway. People will begin to look at you differently and wonder why you had to tear someone else down just to sell a product. They'll wonder why your product couldn't stand on its own.

Again, I don't believe in tearing others down to get ahead. I believe in promoting what makes your product special. Amplify that. If I'm marketing our Rosemary Mint Oil, I'm going to focus on the benefits of it, show before-and-after photos of people using it, and overall highlight what makes the product great. Not what it does or doesn't do compared to another product. So for this brand to use ours as a point of comparison, especially in such a blatant way, showed how far they were willing to go to try to diminish our success. While it was an attempt to show their superiority, to me, it looked like insecurity.

It isn't like I haven't tried to extend olive branches and connect. I've often reached out and tried to make inroads with other brands in my space but am usually met with silence or open disdain. There are a few who have even refused to speak to me at major events despite my best intentions. A few years ago, Mielle participated in a show called Texture on the Runway during New York Fashion Week. It was an opportunity to create innovative segments where models would walk down the runway wearing textured hair. My team and I came up with this Queen of the Jungle theme where the five models—representing the five textured hair brands who were participating—would have their bodies painted in animal print. The symbolism was that the beauty industry is a jungle with everyone fighting for their territory. There's always this assumption that there is a king or queen of the jungle, but I wanted to turn that notion on its head. At first, I walked the runway as the "queen," but then at the end of the runway, I turned and placed a crown on each of the other models' heads as Queen Latifah's song "U.N.I.T.Y." played. It was my way of saying we are all queens of this jungle we're in and that there is room for all of us to rule. And even with all of that, some of those same brand owners still refused to acknowledge me or the effort. That blew my mind! I will never believe we have to treat each other badly or tear each other down in order to succeed.

Despite all the rejections, I haven't let any of it change who I am. In every instance, I've never retaliated; I've always stayed focused. My tunnel vision has become a kind of shelter, one that has allowed Mielle to soar. I encourage you to not let the inevitable arrival of rejection change you. Keep showing up. Keep rooting for others, even when they don't root for you. This is the way of Jesus. To stand ten toes down in your truth no matter what.

This doesn't mean I don't believe in friendly competition. I absolutely do. This is business, after all. But it doesn't have to be so adversarial. I can acknowledge another brand's success, celebrate their wins, and still work to make Mielle the best. I can have a conversation with another owner, even champion her, and still tell her I'm going to beat her at this game. I do that when I play sports with my family. Ask my daughters what I say when we play pickleball: "I love you, but I'm going to beat you." They just laugh, but that's the attitude I try to bring to the industry. Being a smart business owner means knowing what my competitive landscape looks like. But if I see another owner on the street, they're still human. They're still another Black woman whom I respect and admire—someone I wouldn't mind breaking bread with.

A great example of this is what happened when Beyoncé's hair care brand, Cécred, launched in 2024. The excitement around these products was electric, and I was happy to be invited to her exclusive launch event. I know there are people who look at those pictures of me with other hair care brand leaders at the launch and wonder if any of us felt threatened. I can't speak for anyone else, but I showed up because supporting her didn't take anything away from what I've built. I suppose I could have easily been intimidated because—Beyoncé. I could have let the fear of her hair brand doing better than mine stop me from celebrating another Black beauty brand entering the marketplace. But no, I didn't feel any of that. Two things can be true: Beyoncé has done something amazing, and I'm the queen of hair. I still feel like I offer something Beyoncé doesn't, and she absolutely has something that I can't offer. Neither has to take away from what the other is building. So no, I didn't feel diminished by her success; if anything, I felt inspired. I posted about her event because I wanted to celebrate with her, to show that her success is something we can all be proud of because it's a sign that our community is thriving.

But again, that goes back to confidence. I've come to realize that this kind of mindset takes a level of confidence that not everyone has. As a leader, you must boldly walk in fortitude. You must own what God has given you and allow no thought—yours or someone else's—to steal that from you.

This mentality of "there can only be one" isn't new. It's a mindset that dates back to when enslaved Africans were divided by skin tone, hair texture, and proximity to the master's house. Those who were in the house were often pitted against those who were in the field and taught to believe they were better, that they were the chosen ones, despite the personal horrors they experienced in those hidden rooms. That mentality didn't disappear with the end of slavery. It seeped into our culture, teaching us to see each other as competitors rather than allies. The violent post-Reconstruction years and the Jim Crow era only solidified that messaging. We were falsely led to believe that there would never be enough room for all of us.

So yes, I understand where that mentality comes from, and I feel the weight of it every day. I know what our ancestors went through, how they were torn apart, how they were taught to distrust each other. But I also know that we don't have to keep living that way. We can unravel from those messages. We can choose to break free from those chains and lift each other up. It's not easy, but it's worth it. We're stronger together, and the sooner we realize that, the better off we'll be.

I won't pretend that I'm immune to jealousy, though. It's a natural human response. A way our brains and bodies try to keep us safe when we emotionally feel like something is going to be taken from us. There will be times when you will see someone else drop a new product or do the thing you always wanted to do, and you might feel the pang of envy. But when you feel that, remind yourself that there's enough for all of us. Shut that thing down and turn immediately to God in prayer. Ask Him to reverse your thinking so you can stay on track.

It's critical to swiftly combat jealousy when it rises up in us. Turn that "Why them?" into "Good for them!" Even if you don't feel it, you must say it. If you find yourself in naysayer shoes, it might be uncomfortable, but keep saying, "I'm happy for them. I'm proud of them." Eventually, you'll silence the voices of envy and bitterness. Listen, here's the secret: When you clap for others, you aren't just supporting them; you are reinforcing your own faith in the path God has given you. Remember, God is no respecter of persons. If He did it for someone else, what makes you different? What makes you think He won't do it for you?

It's easy to get caught up in comparison, especially in this industry. But it is, without a doubt, a trap. I've been guilty of playing the comparison game, asking myself, *Why didn't they give that to me?* But once again, I check myself immediately. Because usually the answers to my questions are pretty straightforward: I didn't get "that" because God has something else for me. It didn't belong to me. And now it's time to return my eyes to my own paper.

I think that's the biggest problem with naysayers. They are unable to focus on themselves. They follow or study someone they admire so much that they start to subconsciously, or maybe even intentionally, try to mimic what that person is doing. Of course, that rarely works, so then they turn that frustration into confrontation. It becomes "I can't stand that person or brand." Never mind that they don't quite know why they feel the way they do. But the solution is simple, though maybe not easy if you've been a naysayer most of your life. To bring yourself out of such a negative mindset, you must shift your attention to the work of being your authentic self. Focus on *you*. Focus on developing *your* gifts. Investing more time in yourself means you're spending less time worrying about what someone else is or isn't doing. When all you're thinking about is, *How can I do what she did?* you're not doing yourself any good. Instead, ask yourself, *What do I have to offer the world? How do You want to use me, God?* Let God refocus you and return you to who *you* were created to be. Let Him remind you that you don't need to be a naysayer or to chase after someone else's blessings. Yours are on the way.

We can build our businesses and still root for each other. We can pursue any dream we have alongside other dreamers. There is power in unity and strength in numbers. Consider this as you do what you feel called to do. It's time that we all break free from the chains of comparison and scarcity that have held us back for so long. Let's build each other up and show the world what we can do when we come together. We don't have to be each other's enemies. We can choose to be each other's cheerleaders. Because when someone else wins, it means you are one step closer to your own victory.

> **We don't have to be each other's enemies. We can choose to be each other's cheerleaders.**

QUESTIONS FOR REFLECTION

- Reflect on how you support others in your industry or community. Are you able to celebrate their wins without feeling threatened or envious? If not, what steps can you take to genuinely support others while also staying focused on your path?

- Think about moments when you've fallen into the trap of comparison. How did they impact your progress and your mindset? What strategies can you use to focus more on your unique gifts and purpose, rather than on others' successes?

13

Finding Your People

Guiding Principle:
Set boundaries and build a compatible team.

IN ADDITION TO HAVING POSITIVE PARTNERSHIPS AND fruitful collaborations, it's necessary to build a trustworthy team to support your vision. What happens *inside* your business, organization, or home matters just as much as who you are connected to outside of it. The heart of entrepreneurship is not only about launching a product or service; it's about building something that requires a reliable and steadfast group of people who will invest in the growth of your vision. They may not be part owners or investors in the traditional sense, but they are the backbone of your organization. Mielle's success wasn't solely because of my efforts or Melvin's. It was because of the people, both employees and friends, who surrounded us—those who shared my dreams, supported me, and helped cultivate the business into what it is today. But that took time and much trial and error to create.

I remember thinking when I first started the company, *If I could just find the right people, everything would fall into place.* And that was partially true. Finding a good team and building a network of support is necessary, both in business and life. However, discerning good friendships *and* business connections is not always easy. Compatibility, in both personal and professional relationships, is crucial and often underestimated.

One of the biggest challenges I faced early on in "finding my people" is that too often I encountered those who overpromised and underdelivered. I needed people on our team who aligned with our vision, and there were plenty who, theoretically, believed in what we were trying to do. They were talented, had great potential, and promised us the world. But when it came down to what they were willing to give, what they really knew how to do, and how they were going to show up, things got messy. To put it in relational language, they were trying to casually date Mielle but weren't really interested in the long-term commitment. I don't mean to overuse the metaphor of looking for a romantic relationship, but that's exactly what hiring at the management level and above has often felt like: a series of first dates that I hoped worked out. After meeting several potential suitors, it became exhausting because all I really wanted was to find my person. Sometimes I did. Sometimes I didn't.

It's difficult to discern who should be in your personal inner circle. It's even more challenging to do this for a business. You won't always get it right, so give yourself some grace. You're going to hire some people and later find yourself thinking, *What the heck did I just do?* I've hired people who I had to let go within thirty days because they weren't working out. It became clear they weren't in alignment. And I had to be okay with that. As hard as that was, I had to do what's best for Mielle. There's a saying, "Be slow to hire and quick to fire," that has held true for me. There's no rush to hire people. Do the due diligence necessary to make sure you are bringing on someone who is going to serve your vision well. Make sure you're calling those references. I also like to take referrals and recommendations, because it's always good to have a trusted source. A lot of the good people I've hired came through referrals. But again, even in those instances, you will make mistakes. Consider it a learning experience. Each wrong hire brought me closer to understanding who I do and don't want on my team.

Surprisingly, the biggest lesson I've learned in finding and nurturing a trustworthy team is something that goes against my guarded nature and has never been easy for me: We must try to trust people until they give us a reason not to. I speak to so many entrepreneurs who say, "I don't trust people. I don't trust that they're going to get it done the way I like it done." I used to think the same way because so much of how I viewed the world was shaped by childhood trauma. However, I had to learn to reverse that mindset. While my instinct is to be distrustful, I've realized that entering any relationship with my walls up and an expectation that a person is going to hurt me can cause me to miss out on connecting with people who could genuinely help me and my business grow.

As an entrepreneur, as a visionary, it's your responsibility to share the vision clearly. To lay out your expectations from the start. If someone can't buy into your mission or meet your expectations, then they're not the right fit for you. But you won't know whether they can meet (and even exceed) your vision if you enter the relationship with a chip already on your shoulder. That said, you do have to find people who align with the bigger picture you're creating.

One thing I've done to build a strong team in business is to look beyond skill sets when hiring. Of course, you want someone who is competent, but in the same way I do when looking for a partner or collaborator, I also check a potential team member's character. I ask questions that help me understand their moral compass and whether they are in agreement with the culture and values of my company. In my experience, if someone doesn't share my core values, they won't last long. I've hired people who were highly skilled but had poor character, and that kind of mismatch can be toxic to a company's culture. I can teach skills, but I can't change the core of who a person is.

One time I hired someone who, on paper, seemed perfect. They were talented and had all the right qualifications, but there was something about their energy that didn't sit right with me. I also noticed that wherever they went, drama followed. They brought a weirdly depressing energy into any room they were in. I could sense the disharmony, and it very quickly became clear they weren't a good fit.

It could have been that the Spirit of Christ present in my space agitated whatever they were bringing into it. Sometimes that discomfort makes people feel like they need to create drama and confusion. But let me tell you, that kind of behavior wasn't going to last long in our organization. We have a culture of peace and purpose, and anything that disrupts it isn't tolerated for long.

And so I let them go.

Now there are some entrepreneurs who would argue that the most important consideration in the hiring process should be what skills a team member can bring to the organization. The bottom line is the bottom line, so to speak. They would probably suggest I not get too personal or concern myself with an individual's personality or values. But I submit that finding a person with the right degree and work experience is easy. What's not so easy is finding someone whose values align with yours. You can't keep people around just because they're good at what they do.

There have been times when I've hired someone because I wanted to give them a chance, even if there was something about their character that didn't quite feel right or if they had a gap in their skill set. I don't think there's anything wrong with extending compassion and grace in that way. However, if that person starts to show that they aren't ready to rise to the occasion, you can't be afraid to let them go. Just like we wouldn't allow mold to sit on one piece of fruit until it infects the whole, we can't let a toxic personality linger in our business. It's essential to protect the health of the organization by addressing issues before they spread.

This lesson doesn't just apply to business, though. It's true in every aspect of life. Who we allow into our personal space affects our peace and, ultimately, our ability to thrive. When I think back to the moments in my life when I held on to personal relationships that weren't good for me—friendships that seemed beneficial but ultimately drained me—I'm reminded of just how much character and energy matter. Yes, it's very difficult to let someone go. Especially if it's a person you love and care for. But sometimes you must choose peace over familiarity. The same is true in business. If someone is disrupting the flow, it's better to let them go sooner rather than later. Time is your most valuable asset, and you can't afford to waste it.

But when you do find the right fit—someone who aligns with your values, has strong skills, and you can see them being part of your team long-term—you must cultivate that relationship. You need to invest in and nurture the people who are serving your vision. At Mielle, we made it a priority to do team-building activities outside of work. We wanted to get to know our employees beyond just their job roles. We often asked about their families and home lives, and tried to show

Who we allow into our personal space affects our peace and, ultimately, our ability to thrive.

that we cared about them as individuals, not just as employees. Even now, although the company has over three hundred employees and I'm not able to touch every single person every day, I do try to chat with people at, say, a holiday event so I can get to know them. I don't want them to see me as some intimidating CEO. Then and now, I've always wanted to create a family environment where people feel comfortable letting their hair down but still respect me as the boss and leader. There are certain lines I am not willing to cross, but I have always tried to establish a strong connection with the team through work outings or dinners.

But even in this, there were lessons to be learned.

———

As a business leader, you have to put boundaries in place. I can assure you, when you go against those boundaries, you will likely regret it. For example, because I'd built such good relationships with my team, I made the mistake of inviting them to my home once or twice. I had a rule early on that I wouldn't allow employees into my personal space—my home. I felt it was important to keep a clear boundary between my professional life and my personal life. However, as the company grew and our relationships deepened, I let that boundary slip. I invited a few key employees over, thinking it wouldn't hurt.

Boy, did I regret that!

That level of personal familiarity started to blur the lines between professionalism and friendship. It complicated the CEO–employee dynamic. Suddenly, employees began treating me more like their "homegirl" than their boss, and that familiarity made it difficult to maintain the level of respect necessary for a leader–employee relationship. People who once admired me from afar now wanted all-inclusive access to my time, my resources, and even my personal life. Others tried to connect with me for the wrong reasons.

As Mielle grew, and we secured partnership deals with investment companies like New Voices and Berkshire, it was even more crucial to set those boundaries. My schedule became incredibly busy—in a good way. Or so I thought. Before, we had an open-door policy where people could walk into the office whenever they wanted. We always wanted to create an environment where people felt comfortable, like they could come to us and talk if they really needed to. But that open-door policy turned out to be both a gift and a curse. People started walking into the office whenever, even if I was in the middle of something important—whether it was responding to an email or on a Zoom call. There was this sense that because we had created such an open environment, people felt like they could interrupt at any time.

I started to realize that people weren't respecting my time. I had to be in the office. I had major responsibilities in running this company. And yet people were walking in as if it was a casual conversation space. It got to the point where I had to make changes. We had to implement systems. Now I have an assistant who acts as the gatekeeper, scheduling meetings and managing my calendar. Some people didn't like that. They felt like

I had changed, that I was no longer accessible. But the truth is, I had to evolve to meet the demands of my role.

If I didn't maintain control of something as simple as my time, then I would, in essence, end up letting people run my schedule. That was and is not sustainable at the level I was trying to grow the business. When I didn't set these boundaries around my availability in the office, I couldn't get my work done. I ended up frustrated and overwhelmed because it felt like people were taking advantage of me.

Never let anyone dictate your life and schedule. As a CEO (of a business or in a particular area of life), you're likely in high demand, and many people need your attention. I've learned that when someone requests my time, they often feel like they're the only person asking me for that one thing. They don't realize that there may be twenty other people asking for the same thing that week. They don't understand that they aren't the only ones who need my attention.

If I didn't set those boundaries and continued to let all those requests control my time, running at everyone's beck and call, I would inevitably burn out. Again, I'd be frustrated and overwhelmed, and I wouldn't even know why. But, deep down, we do know why, don't we? The reason we feel the way we do in those moments is that we've tried to be everything to everyone, and that's simply impossible. You have to be mentally whole and sound for yourself first. If you don't put policies in place, you're setting yourself up for failure. You're setting your team up for failure. I knew that if I didn't set guidelines for how I chose to work, for what worked best for me, then having thousands of people needing something from me would mean I would not get anything done.

So I pulled back. I am warm and friendly by nature, but that doesn't automatically mean I will allow people to overstep. It doesn't mean that I am going to ignore the times when the lines between personal and professional relationships have quickly blurred and not self-correct. You must be vigilant about maintaining boundaries because, without them, the roles become confused. And confusion in roles can lead to breakdowns in communication, performance, and, ultimately, the business itself.

Sadly, when I began removing certain levels of access people thought they had, things got complicated. It had to happen, but they were not happy about it. I started hearing, "Oh, I thought we were cool. I thought I could just . . ." No, I was still the boss. Then people accused me of acting different. No, I wasn't "acting funny" or "acting different." It hurt to hear that. But it was always and only about setting boundaries. I had to conduct myself in a way that matched the new responsibilities I carried. I haven't achieved my accomplishments by staying the same. I've had to grow and adapt to new situations.

And at the end of the day, I still sign their paychecks. I still have to make tough decisions as their boss. So I don't want those lines to be blurred. I'm not their friend. We may work together, and we're building something great together, but we're not best friends. I've hired them to do a job, and that's the relationship I need to maintain. Yes, that feels harsh. But it's the bottom-line truth. I think so many of those early employees confused the warmth and friendliness Melvin and I brought into the environment with being something deeper than it was. They took that kindness and tried to take advantage of it, thinking it meant they had more access than was appropriate.

Friend, if you plan to scale your business, ministry, or career opportunities beyond your current level, then it's inevitable you will face this same dilemma as you grow. You'll want to be accessible, to maintain that sense of camaraderie and openness with your team, but there will come a point when you will have to protect your own sanity, including your time and energy, for the good of the business. A tried-and-true, trustworthy team member will understand that. They will understand that someone in a leadership position is often pulled in different directions, and if they don't set those boundaries, it's likely they will not make sound decisions for the business. That's not good for anyone. You see, setting those boundaries isn't just about protecting yourself; it's about ensuring that you have the capacity to lead effectively. For me, I always ask myself, *Does this add value to my life or business? Does this align with my future goals?* And if the thing I'm considering doesn't, then I have no problem with saying no. It might be uncomfortable. And people might not understand. But when I am clear about my boundaries, the right people will stay, and the wrong ones will naturally fall away.

Years ago, I read something that has helped me tremendously: "Boundaries are never something someone else has to enforce. They are solely about what you do."[1] When you set a boundary, you're saying, "This is what I'm going to do if you cross this line," or "This is what I'm going to put in place to prevent you from crossing that line. This is how I'm going to respond to protect myself." The other person then has to decide whether or not they'll honor that boundary.

Sometimes we mistakenly set boundaries that imply, "You need to do this, or you need to do that," when really, a boundary is about you and your actions. For example, with my team, I've had to say, "If you need to speak with me, please contact my assistant to schedule an appointment." That's the boundary. And as an entrepreneur, I've had to grieve the reality that some people, with whom I've otherwise had a good relationship, may not respect or be able to handle that boundary—and I might have to let them go because of it.

I suppose the lesson here is that boundaries matter more than we like to think when trying to nurture the team we have built. When you compromise your boundaries, it will actually create more problems for you in the long run than if you had simply stuck with them. It's so much harder to un-ring a bell. People's feelings will be hurt when you decide to create or reinforce boundaries after the fact. Nevertheless, do it. As a leader, if you don't set those expectations from the start or add them when you realize things have gone off the rails, people will begin to feel entitled, and that entitlement can lead to problems.

––––––

Part of being a great team member is having the ability to balance that space between knowing your worth and feeling entitled. I've had team members who began to feel they were entitled to a certain position or a certain level of pay without having to work for it. And while many had the will to grow in the company, they didn't necessarily have the skill set for the position they were trying to obtain. But instead of being humble and saying, "Hey, I'd really like XYZ position. What do you suggest I do to gain the skills for that level of responsibility? What can I learn in order to be better suited for that role?" they just up and quit the company because they felt like we were not giving them their due justice by promoting them.

And it honestly feels worse as a Black-owned company. If an employee at Pepsi was told by their boss that they still had more training to do or more skills to develop, most people would start taking those classes and doing what was necessary to be promoted—without question. But for some reason there is an interesting familiarity—or maybe it's indignity—some people feel when that same suggestion is given by a Black CEO. It's like they think that if I'm in my position, they deserve a higher position too. If I drive a certain car, they should be driving that kind of car too. Which, of course, implies that I do not deserve to be in my position or to have what I have.

It's my experience that people who have this kind of spirit of arrogance or entitlement rarely change. I do not like to generalize, but that's been my observation. Their MO is to monitor the moves and actions of everyone else as opposed to being self-aware about what they are bringing to the table—not what they *imagine* they are bringing. Unfortunately, each time Mielle hit certain milestones, the level of entitlement we experienced from some who worked for us increased. The hard truth is, these individuals didn't make the sacrifices I did. Nor did I ever ask them to. They didn't go without pay as Melvin and I did on many occasions. Nor did I expect them to. And yet, they expected to reap the same benefits, if not more, that we did as the owners of the company, who actually took the risks and made the sacrifices.

This is the reason we became very intentional about not giving numbers when we did our major partnership deals and, especially, when we sold the company to Procter & Gamble. When we had received our investment infusion from Berkshire Partners in 2021, we publicized a general amount but nothing exact. But eventually, we couldn't keep those numbers from some of our employees, especially those at the executive level, or C-suite as it's called. So as soon as word got out, the phone calls were like a tidal wave with asks coming in hard and fast. There were some on our team who we quickly learned weren't there to be part of a team at all. They weren't thinking that everyone had come together to do their jobs, which had translated into the increase. They believed we would not have accomplished what we did without them. Which, even in my gratitude for the work they did, I knew was not true.

Here's a hard truth in business that these individuals, and many people, do not get: Everyone is replaceable. Even me.

I don't say that to be mean or disrespectful. I say that to emphasize the fact that if a person leaves any position in corporate America today, either willingly or unwillingly, it will not be long before that position will be filled again. We can argue all day about the "rightness" of that, but this is the reality. It wasn't just one person in particular who took us from $50 million to $100 million. It wasn't even just me or Melvin who contributed. It was a team effort. And I can guarantee if there was anyone on the team who couldn't do the job, there was always someone else waiting in the proverbial wings who could.

———

Which brings me to a point I made in the previous chapter: Just like outside business partners, members of your team might not be part of your journey long-term. Even friendships might only last for a season. This is why it's important to not only find your people but to continue to periodically evaluate whether they are *still* your people. Discern who fits into each category of your life, because not every friendship or business connection is meant to last forever. One of the hardest things in life—particularly in entrepreneurship—is recognizing when it's time to let a person go. In fact, even more important than finding people who are good for you is learning to let go of those who are not. This has been a recurring theme in my life, both personally and professionally. Sometimes we hold on to people longer than we should because we don't want to hurt their feelings or because we're afraid of being alone. But what I've learned is that letting go is not a loss; it's a necessary step for growth.

I've had to let go of people I once thought were going to be with me for the long haul. It is one of the hardest things I've ever had to do. But I've learned that in order to grow, you sometimes have to prune the branches.

When we lost so many critical employees after doing that Berkshire deal, it was hard. It wasn't all entitlement. It was just a matter of people needing to move on. That happens. They were with us for a season, and God revealed to one or both of us that our season together was over. But there were others whose entire character changed—to the extent that I found myself thinking, *Wow, I didn't see this coming. Is this the real you? Was this the real you from the very beginning and you were trying to get this experience under your belt just to say you worked for Mielle? Were you just trying to get an inside look to see how we did it so you can do something similar?* And I learned that my thoughts weren't far-fetched. There were those who only worked for us to leverage the Mielle brand name or even to eventually start a similar company as us—despite any noncompetes we might have had in place.

This is why I am so grateful that our faith was at the center of everything we did. Because there were days when I surely needed to remind myself of that. In fact, I never forgot the meeting we had with our pastor early on in the business when he told us that with success comes persecution. In only a few years after that meeting, he would be proven right.

Let me clear this up for you so you can go find your people with eyes wide open. The more you grow, the bigger and more successful your business gets, the more you will be persecuted. People will try to attack you. They will spread rumors about you. They will try to sabotage your business with lies. Some will approach you, pretending to be happy for you, but will have ulterior motives. It will turn out that they weren't being genuine; they simply wanted something from you.

For instance, those higher-level team members who were disgruntled after the Berkshire deal? Many of them talked bad about us. But what they didn't know was that we were preparing to offer them equity in the deal. Which might not have been the quick hit to grab the cool ride they wanted so they could feel like they were on the same playing field as us. But do you know how much that equity would have been worth after we sold the company to Procter & Gamble?

Let's just say . . . a lot!

Yet, of those we were going to offer equity to, most of them left before the deal even closed. Ninety percent left equity on the table because of their entitled egos and the feeling that they should have a certain position or certain levels of access. They chose a title over the possibility of significant equity in a business that has now been scaled and sold to one of the largest companies on the planet.

I couldn't understand it at the time. I said to Melvin, "They have an opportunity to change their lives and their family's lives. But they are going to leave it all on the table because they weren't promoted to a senior director level or president level?"

It made no sense to me.

But in the context of what I now know makes a true and trustworthy team member, it makes perfect sense.

Black folks have been fed lies in a system that tells us the position and titles matter more than the big picture of generational wealth and community building. Because of this, we often find it hard to work together and accumulate wealth because we stay in competition with each other. Some of us focus very narrowly on things that will feed the gaps in our self-worth and our need for status as opposed to really thinking about what kind of legacy we want to leave. The latter is always the kind of team member I look for. I want the big-picture thinkers on my team.

I had a talk with my spiritual mentor, Andria Hudson, when all of this was happening, because it was really affecting me. I couldn't understand why these people were leaving the way they were. I felt like we all worked well together as a team. Everyone said that Mielle felt like a family environment, yet they were leaving the company. In a way, it felt like they were leaving me. But Andria helped me understand that this was possibly God's way of removing those who would not be able to go to the next level. She helped me take my emotions out of the equation and see everything through a more levelheaded business lens. The people who might have helped us get to $50 million were not necessarily going to be the same people to help us get to $100 million.

That said, people matter. I firmly believe people are more important than progress. Compassion, empathy, and humanity must lead the way. It can't be about *just* the bottom line or making a dollar, because when you focus on taking care of people, everything else—growth, success, progress—naturally follows. But you do need people who will believe in your vision. And not everyone will be your person. That's okay. But that doesn't mean you compromise your heart or integrity. I've learned that when you lead with good intentions and a servant mindset—focusing on serving others first—you can't go wrong.

This brings me back to the importance of compatibility. This is not something that only applies to romantic relationships. It's important in friendships and especially in business. You should be intentional about the relationships you're cultivating. As I've said, it's not enough to surround yourself with people who are talented; they have to be the right people with the right mindset and the right intentions for you and your business.

I am grateful for the lessons I've learned about relationships, boundaries, and compatibility. Every mistake, every wrong hire, every difficult conversation has brought me closer to understanding what it means to build something that lasts. Personally and professionally, people play a huge role in how far you can go. No one achieves success alone, and the quality of the people around you will determine how high you rise or how fast you fall. You need people who believe in you, who will hold you accountable, and who will be there to support you through the ups and downs. Whether it's an employee, a mentor, or a friend, these relationships are invaluable. They can make or break your success. So choose wisely.

QUESTIONS FOR REFLECTION

- Reflect on the individuals in your personal and professional circles. Are they contributing positively to your growth and purpose, or are they detracting from it? How can you further cultivate relationships with those who genuinely support your journey?
- Think about the ways you establish boundaries to protect your time, energy, and mental health. Are there any areas where you've been hesitant to set limits? If so, how can you take steps to reinforce them?

When Humility Calls

14

Guiding Principle:
Know what you don't know.

THE ONLY WAY TO CREATE GREAT BUSINESS PARTNER-
ships and build a trustworthy team, all while keeping God at the center of
your mission and calling, is by choosing to have a spirit of humility as a
leader. This may be the hardest thing for an entrepreneur to do. We tend
to be naturally ambitious visionaries who have a clear understanding of
what we are trying to accomplish and difficulty letting other people in
enough to delegate some of what we need to grow. We mistakenly believe
that true humility makes us appear small. Inconsequential. We see it as
a position of weakness because a distorted version of "humbleness" has
been weaponized against us by those who don't want to see a woman or
a Black person succeed. But that's not true humility.

There is a difference between being humble and being humbled. The
first is a choice you make as you recognize your humanity. The latter is
either the result of your poor decision-making or a tool others will use
to dehumanize you. For me, humility is about simply acknowledging my
limitations and being confident enough to fill those gaps with people and

resources that will help me and my business grow. It is the single most important trait needed to grow a business or a family, or even to simply maintain some semblance of harmony in the middle of life's chaos. Humility is also a spiritual practice for me that goes hand in hand with my faith.

The Bible reminds us that God gives grace to the humble, not the proud (James 4:6). His grace is a powerful resource to draw upon when we are trying to build anything of importance. As a believer, I'm called to a life of learning and growth. Jesus Himself exemplified humility as He grew in wisdom and stature. He was not afraid to listen and to serve despite knowing full well who He was and what God was bringing into the earth through Him. People saw the overall gentleness of Christ and tried to exploit that, but He remained steadfast in His mission. I find that having a spirit of humility has meant that I maintain a hunger for learning and service that aligns me with Jesus' example.

I also take very seriously when the Bible says, "Pride goes before destruction, and a haughty spirit before a fall" (Proverbs 16:18 ESV). It's a reminder that arrogance—which, unfortunately, many entrepreneurs struggle with—only leads to failure. When we put ourselves above others, we lose sight of God's call to love and serve. I've seen many business owners stumble because they think they have it all figured out. They refuse to lean on others, let alone God, for guidance. You can easily get sucked into the mindset, especially as you grow, that no one can do a certain thing better than you can. I struggled with this myself when I first became a nurse. I wouldn't ask for help in the beginning because I had that strong will my mom passed on that said it's not good to ask people for help, or to be seen as a burden. It wasn't until I shifted into building and growing Mielle that I realized if I don't ask for help, I will never grow.

Without humility, you will inevitably close yourself off from the wisdom God has placed in the people around you. Being humble opens doors to growth by allowing us to feel free to ask questions, seek guidance, and, most importantly, say "I don't know." I believe that once you stop learning, you stop growing. Having the drive to ask all the right questions is what initiates your growth, but it's the humility to truly listen to the answers that will take your vision to the next level.

Humility will allow you to create a business environment where you can trust others to help make decisions. It gives you the ability to make room for a team to feel valued, knowing they can offer advice, express concerns, and give input that will be genuinely considered. People often tell me that I'm a good listener. Again, in meetings, I'm never going to be the loudest person or the one doing most of the talking. I tend to sit quietly, absorbing and taking in all the information. Surrounding yourself with people who have greater expertise and experience shows that you are okay with not having all the answers—because they just might.

My mentor Germaine always told me, "Yes, this is your vision, but the vision doesn't come from just your two eyes. It comes from all the people around you whom you've put in place to support you, based on their knowledge and expertise." She was basically saying that God puts people in our lives to support our vision and to guide us with their gifts, and they are just as much a part of the execution of that vision as we are. So if I've trusted someone enough to put them in a particular position, then why not trust my own judgment about their expertise? They're likely telling me something worthwhile that will benefit the business in the long run.

There's that word again: trust! Proverbs 15:22 doesn't mince words: "Plans fail for lack of counsel, but with many advisers they succeed." It doesn't get much clearer than that. I've learned the same over these ten years of doing business: Wisdom comes from having a multitude of counselors.

Even when we did the deal with Berkshire, one of the key reasons they said they believed in us was because they saw that we were "two individuals who have a hunger for knowledge." We were coachable. Our willingness to listen made us stand out as a business they wanted to invest in. We were very clear about our strengths and weaknesses, and we weren't afraid to admit where we needed help. Of course, we also were not naive. We weren't going to let people walk all over us or manipulate us. But having a spirit of humility allowed us to be teachable, to grow, and to accept guidance without losing our sense of purpose.

Meanwhile, you have some CEOs who insist that they're good at everything and so they'll do everything. They'll work their social media accounts *and* do their bookkeeping. They'll create products *and* handle shipping. That's hard. Mostly because doing everything often means doing things that require the opposite sides of your brain at any given moment. It's rare to find people who can effectively operate with both.

Yes, in the beginning it's inevitable that an entrepreneur will wear many hats. I'm not speaking necessarily to the early years. I'm speaking about individuals who can delegate but choose not to. When an entrepreneur attempts to do everything, it's highly likely they will end up sacrificing the most important things—the things that *do* require just them. Instead of getting someone to help with social media marketing, they will find themselves posting all day instead of writing their strategic plan. Instead of hiring an accountant, they will spend critical time scanning receipts instead of working on their pitch presentation for funding.

Berkshire was able to quickly assess our strengths, which, in turn, empowered us to operate with excellence. My strengths were setting the vision, product innovation, understanding ingredients, and knowing how I wanted the products to perform for our consumers. I understood the science behind our products and how to communicate the benefits in a way that resonated with our audience. Because I was good at connecting with people, Berkshire's investment allowed me to offload tasks that took up a lot of my time but weren't as effective for the brand.

They helped us split up our roles so we could focus on what truly drives the business. They quickly saw that Melvin was strong in operations, logistics, and finance. So they restructured our org chart to put all finance and operations under his leadership, while innovation, marketing, and PR fell under mine. But for any of this to work, we had to be open and coachable enough to hear them say, "This is how we're going to help you succeed. Here's how we'll divvy up responsibilities so you can focus and excel where you're strongest." And as the visionary for the company, I had to be humble enough to step back and let Melvin and others lead where they were strongest. In my mind, the model for this was, once again, Jesus. He sent His disciples out two by two, each with specific roles. No one was expected to carry the load alone. Similarly, I was not meant to carry every responsibility; I was meant to share it with those God has placed in my path.

What many entrepreneurs don't realize is that having humility requires a level of self-awareness that I believe only comes from a deep relationship with God. Can you trust God? Can you trust yourself? Can you trust the people God has sent to help you? God created us as part of a larger body, with different gifts meant to complement each other. Trying to do it all is not only exhausting but also a way of telling God, "I don't trust You or anyone else." Being clear on what I'm good at and delegating the rest isn't about avoiding responsibility; it's about stewarding the resources and people God has entrusted to me.

———

Most entrepreneurs learn quickly that they cannot grow a business without being humble enough to partner with people who can do what they can't—or can do things better. Mielle received so much flack for scaling our business in stages and eventually partnering with P&G. But I think people forget that the natural progression of building a global beauty brand led by Black people will require partnership at some level. I've spoken with founders—even those who are believers—who have out-and-out resisted input from investors because they feel like it's theirs; they created it. Fine. But know this: There's a price to pay for holding on too tightly to something that God may have called to be bigger than you can imagine. It's okay if you don't want to bring on investors, as long as you understand that you will limit the capacity of your business at some point. You cannot scale unless you are willing to let go and trust people to help your vision grow.

Some entrepreneurs will go as far as to have investors come in, but when those same investors offer much-needed advice, they say, "I'm not going to do this because . . ." Granted, there are times when you need to stick to your guns on things that are essential for the brand. But you also have to be willing to compromise sometimes and find common ground. Having investors is a lot like being in a marriage; whoever you work with will have their own thoughts and ideas. Have your nonnegotiables—for us, that meant keeping the formulas unchanged—but also stay open-minded in the areas that can be improved.

I believe this is what Germaine was getting at when she said that the vision doesn't just come from my two eyes; it comes from the people I've employed to help scale the dream. You can't scale by being small-minded. You scale by having a growth mindset, and that means asking a lot of questions. To this day, I'm going to learn as much as I can to help grow this business to the level I know it can reach.

If you are a believer, it's even more important to be open to the ideas and input of others. Remember, our faith teaches us to value the collective. "As iron sharpens iron, so one person sharpens another" (Proverbs 27:17). God calls us to grow ourselves and, I submit, anything we are involved in, through the building of relationships. And those relationships require the willingness to listen and collaborate. This is the essence of humility—to recognize that the vision is bigger than any one person. It's a collective perspective shaped by a God who loves community.

Having humility also allows us to see most people as possible mentors or teachers, not threats. Before P&G and Berkshire, and before becoming immersed in the world of venture capitalism, Melvin and I still understood the power of tapping the expertise of those who were doing what we wanted to do. When I met Rich, who, as you might remember, was the owner of the hugely popular Shea Moisture hair brand, I made my intentions clear: "I want to do what you did, but better." I'm sure he probably thought, *This girl is crazy*, but he's a pretty laid-back guy, so I felt comfortable saying that, knowing he'd understand what I meant.

We ended up having a great and promising conversation about business and our industry that day. But he didn't become my mentor or investor right away. It wasn't until later, after he sold Shea Moisture to Unilever, that we got the opportunity to work together. After the sale, he created the New Voices Fund as a way to invest in Black women entrepreneurs. He also purchased *Essence*, a storied and respected magazine for Black women that had for many years been owned by the publishing conglomerate Time Warner. Rich received so much criticism for selling his Black-owned business, and yet he showed his true colors when he turned the resources he gained from the sale of Shea Moisture into an opportunity to "buy back" one of the Black community's stalwart publications. *That's* the power of scaling.

Three years after that initial meeting, when Mielle was actively looking for investors, I reminded Rich of that first conversation. I told him, "I'm looking for an investor because I want to—even more so now—do what you've done. I want to learn from you. I want to know the roadmap."

I encourage you to never be too intimidated to approach someone super successful in their industry and say, "Teach me." That approach takes a spirit of humility. If I'd approached Rich arrogantly, I would have seen him as my competitor, thinking, *I'm going to be better than you, and I'm going to do it my own way because I know everything.* But I saw him as someone who had achieved what I hoped to accomplish.

We don't win by competing with a crabs-in-the-barrel mentality. We win by sharing knowledge and information. The multicultural hair care space holds a very small percentage of retail shelf space in comparison to other beauty brands. If we are constantly looking at each other as competition, then we're essentially fighting over crumbs. But if we come together, leveraging what all of us have done, we can create something magnificent. That changes the narrative. As a result, we're creating more opportunities for people who look like us. We become the conglomerates who reinvest back into our communities.

If I'd had that crabs-in-the-barrel mentality or a spirit of arrogance instead of humility, I would never have approached Rich that day. Nor would I have sought him out three years later. And I probably wouldn't have accomplished what I have. He was a mentor who showed me the blueprint, and when Mielle sold to P&G, he was one of the early investors who benefitted as well.

———

I'd be lying if I didn't say that having a spirit of humility can make you a bit of a target. People will try to exploit you or your business. They will think they can get over on you because they see your willingness to learn and hear other ideas and believe that makes you weak. But don't worry about those folks. There is power in being underestimated. It allows you to move strategically.

People try to take my kindness for weakness all the time, but if I'm honest, I like being underestimated. Mostly because I know that my strength—and the strength of the Lord—will ultimately shut down any shenanigans. There was one time when a man, a well-known public figure, presented a business deal to us. He asked my husband if he wanted to co-invest. Melvin, always eager to help, said to me, "I'm going to invest in this up-and-coming entrepreneur. It seems like a good business venture." Unfortunately, it turned out to be a scam. It wasn't even a real business. All the paperwork he'd shown my husband was fake. When Melvin should have started seeing returns on his investment, there was nothing. He reached out to the man, asking about the payout, and that's when the lies began to unravel.

First, we heard that the business owner was in the hospital with COVID and on life support. It was sad news, and we felt compassion, reaching out to others to get more information. But after a few conversations, something didn't feel right. My radar went up, and I thought, *Something is strange with this situation.* Melvin contacted someone who was supposed to be the man's power of attorney but got nowhere.

I suppose this person thought we wouldn't do anything about being scammed. Maybe he believed that because they were cool with us, we would just write off the money as a loss. But they underestimated us. We contacted our attorneys and began the process of suing this person. As of this writing, there's a lien on his house and a judgment against his name.

Having humility in business doesn't mean you're a sucker. It means you're open to working with people who are gifted in areas where you might not be. Humility was the reason why we didn't go on social media to tarnish this man's character. We didn't feel the need to. I believe God sees all. He sees the harm that people might attempt to do to you, so we can trust that He will fight your battles.

Allowing humility to lead can be challenging, especially when you've been burned before for trusting someone. But God calls us to community, to relationships, to openness, so the answer isn't to shut down your humility when you've been taken advantage of. The answer is to be sure that your humility lives alongside your discernment. These two operate together so that the decisions you ultimately make will align with what God has ordained. I pray for discernment every single day. And when I pray for discernment, I also pray that God gives me the wisdom to know what to do with what I'm discerning.

In the case of this business scam, and with any other person we've had issues with, there were definitely warning signs. Sometimes we ignore them because we want to give people a chance. We want to be for them what Rich and others have been for us. But again, every time we have gone against our gut, we have ended up regretting it. Every single time. God has given us that built-in radar, a sense of knowing when something is off. So in any encounter with someone, try to pay attention to that inner voice and trust that it's God guiding you. When you do this, then you can afford to be humble, to delegate, and to collaborate because you'll always know that God is pouring His wisdom into you.

It's true what they say: new levels, new devils. The higher we go, the more our humility will be tested. The higher we climb, the more we must rely on God to keep us grounded. Even when we're doing our best to leave things in God's hands, there's a kind of hypervigilance we have to maintain when we reach a certain level of success. I have to work really hard at not being too guarded—not retreating into myself and trying to do it all because I feel people can't be trusted.

God created us for community, and healthy relationships are our portion.

I believe there are still good people in the world, don't you? So let us remind ourselves daily that God created us for community, and healthy relationships are our portion. If we are too guarded and lack humility, we might end up blocking the blessings and healthy relationships God has for us. Humility isn't a business strategy, though. It is a non-negotiable chapter in your life story. It's a way of life that aligns with God's call.

QUESTIONS FOR REFLECTION

- Think about the difference between being humble and being humbled. How can you consciously choose humility in a way that strengthens your faith, empowers your leadership, and honors the gifts of those around you?
- Consider the aspects of your work or personal life where you may have been hesitant to admit a lack of knowledge. How can embracing humility in these areas open you to growth and new opportunities?

15

Keeping the Main Thing
the Main Thing

Guiding Principle:
Grow and attend to what matters most.

IF THERE IS ONE THING STARTING MIELLE HAS TAUGHT
me, it's the importance of adaptation and sustainability—at both the
personal and business level. That said, there are core values and commit-
ments that have remained true for Melvin and me even in the uncertain
ups and downs of being in this industry. From the beginning, we decided
that our priorities would be God, family, and business. And this guiding mission isn't just something we say; it's a practice we live by every
day. God must be at the center of everything. We must make a conscious
effort to involve our family in the business so that they feel like they're a
part of what we're building. And a huge part of holding family sacred is
also being protective of our marriage. This means not letting anything
come between us, including the business, outside people, outside voices,
and other distractions. Yet, I think this is probably an area that comes
under fire the most. As much as there are people who do not want to see

a successful Black woman thrive, there is an equal number of people who despise seeing a Black couple doing the same. It challenges the stereotypes they've bought into, or they simply cannot believe that our kind of love and ambition can coexist the way it does.

We certainly are not perfect. Our marriage has taken its hits, especially with all the fluctuations and growth our business has had over the last ten years. But we are committed. To each other. To our dreams. We don't want to wake up one day and realize that the only thing we have going for us is this business project. We want to make sure that we're friends first and always. We're intentional about loving each other and prioritizing that love because we know that one day, when our children are grown, it will be just the two of us in the house again. We want to be able to look at each other and feel that we're still friends, still deeply in love.

One of the ways we have been able to nurture our relationship while growing Mielle is by prioritizing quality time together. We don't necessarily stick to a strict schedule for date nights, as our lives and schedules can be chaotic. But we do have our moments.

For instance, when we go out of town for a business meeting, if it's just the two of us, we will sometimes mix business outings with spending quality time together. Outside of that, even if we don't have a set schedule, we do try to make sure that if a month goes by and we haven't gone on a date, we'll randomly say, "Let's go out somewhere." In fact, we do a lot of spontaneous dates. That's what works for us. We rarely have something set in stone. I know some people have Thursday date nights, or whatever, and maybe we'll get there eventually, but with our crazy schedules, we both just know when it's time to reconnect. It's almost better when we don't have something planned. To me, it shows we are being intentional about spending time together, even if it's random.

For special occasions like anniversaries or birthdays, we always make sure to plan at least a getaway or a staycation somewhere. If we can't get away from the house, we'll travel when we can. We make a point to stay in tune with each other's love languages and needs, and we try to be there for each other when it matters most. These moments allow us to reconnect and keep the romance alive. They also remind us that no matter what's going on in the business, all the changes that might be happening around us, even the ways we are growing and changing personally, our love is constant. That's why we attend to it whenever and however we can.

Building this brand together and being purposeful about it has allowed Mel and me to grow closer. Seeing each other evolve—from him being a project engineer at UPS where I didn't really know or understand what he did, from me working as a nurse where he probably didn't fully understand my role—has been a true journey. Then going into business together—where I got to see him take charge and he began seeing me in a new phase of my life—has been eye-opening. He became this strong, intelligent authority figure, and someone I could fall in love with all over again. Similarly, he's watched me evolve from an introverted nurse to an ambitious businesswoman who can hold her own in any room. These transformations—which, for some couples, might have brought out feelings of uncertainty or frustration—have actually drawn us closer to each other. We've both chosen to use those changes to find new ways to admire and love each other.

We've also been blessed to have older, wiser friends who serve as examples and models for a good marriage. Sometimes we joke, "Man, we need to get some younger friends, people our age." But we actually enjoy having older friends, especially older married couples, because we can learn from them. If anything, that's the biggest key to our marital success. They provide positive examples for us, which we didn't have growing up. Neither of us came from a family with strong examples of healthy marriages. We both come from very dysfunctional backgrounds, so having examples of what it takes to make a marriage work, to raise children, and to build a godly family has been incredibly helpful. I recommend this for any couple, but especially those who want to work as closely together as we do in business. As an entrepreneurial couple, you must be willing to find new ways to get to know your partner. If done right, each new discovery allows you to fall in love with that person all over again.

Our pastors, Steve and Melody Munsey, have been key mentors in our lives. They gave us one piece of advice that really stuck: Keep your bedroom your sanctuary. Sometimes Mel would bring the laptop into the room, or I'd be on mine, and we'd both be in bed, checking emails, scrolling through Instagram, and so on. But our pastor said, "Don't do that. Use your bedroom for intimate, private moments and rest only." He explained that mixing work with that space disrupts its sacredness and the intimacy it brings. He told us this about three or four years ago, and since then, we've stuck by that rule and haven't brought a laptop into the room. Now we use our bedroom solely for rest and intimacy. Establishing that as a boundary has helped us maintain a strong connection with each other, even as we've both personally evolved over the years. Every day we are learning how to adapt to each other's needs in order to sustain the mission of our family and business.

———

The dynamics of any personal relationship you have will evolve. It's inevitable. The things we want at twenty years old aren't usually the same things we want when we're older. Melvin and I have decided that this is okay. But as a result, he has had to get to know me anew at this stage of life, and I've had to do the same. Sure, he may not like all the expectations or demands I have now, but at the end of the day, he says, "I'm going to compromise because this is a new version of her. I love her, and I want to make her happy, so I'll adapt to what my wife wants." And, of course, it goes both ways. It's way too easy to get caught up in that negative train of thought, like, *This isn't the person I married. They've changed.* But that's not how you sustain longevity in marriage—or in business, for that matter. Being adaptable is the way.

Melvin and I have also learned a lot about compromise, especially when it comes to those evolving expectations. In the early stages of our relationship, he would only open the car door for me sometimes. Many times he would not. And while I was taught that this was something a man should do for me, I didn't always demand it in my twenties. But later it started to bug me and I communicated to him that this was something I valued. I told him, "You need to open the car door every time. I'm not going to get in unless you open it." Maybe it was becoming a mother of two girls that did it. We both want our daughters to have high standards. I wanted them to be treated in a certain way and knew the only way they would value that treatment was if they saw it acted out by their first love—their dad.

We went back and forth on this. He tried, but sometimes he'd forget because it wasn't yet a habit. If I got in the car without him opening the door, I'd give him a look and roll my eyes, like, *Oh, so you're not going to open the door?* In turn, he'd get frustrated because I wasn't being patient, and I'd get frustrated because he wasn't doing what I wanted.

I think it was hard for Melvin at first to wrap his mind around why this was "all of a sudden" important to me. Many men might find themselves thinking, *Well, this is not something you required back then, so why are you asking for it now?* He eventually accepted the fact that my expectations had changed from when I was in my twenties because that's what happens. We grow. With age, I expect certain things. Different things. Things I might have let slide out of youthful oblivion weren't things I was willing to let slide forever. I wanted him to treat me a certain way, and opening the car door is part of that. Thankfully, after some patience on both our parts, he came around and it became a routine for him to open my door. Now, in the big scheme of things, this is a small issue. But what's bigger is he was willing to adapt to my evolution, and there are many instances where I've had to do the same. That's what matters most to me. Neither of us will always get it right, but at least we show each other that we're listening and that we care.

———

Another critical part of maintaining our relationship while leading such a fast-growing business in an even faster-growing industry has been setting boundaries—not as a way to manage the way we engage with other people, as I've discussed previously, but as a way to manage how we engage each other when it comes to what other people may do.

As a married couple in business together, you have to comply and compromise a lot to make things work. That's not easy. Melvin and I have bumped heads often. A large share of our disagreements are about hiring and firing employees. We've had situations where I might be ready to let someone go and find myself wanting to do it immediately. I can get very emotional about these things, and sometimes I expect him to back me up, even when he doesn't agree. But Melvin has taught me to handle tough decisions with grace, and we've created a system to navigate those sticky moments: If there's a personnel decision that needs to be made and I'm very emotional about it, he steps in as the levelheaded one. If he's the emotional one, then I take on that role. We're like yin and yang in that way.

We had one situation where we hired someone who, although we liked her, turned out to be a bad hire. Since she worked under me, I had to be the one to terminate her, but I really didn't want to do it. In fact, I was dreading it. Yes, it's true that all employees are replaceable, but I had taken a liking to this person and didn't want to be the one to do this hard thing of letting her go. Being the calm to my storm, Melvin tried to coach me on what to say and how to handle the situation, but that just upset me more. I told him, "Why don't you just do it? This is your area of expertise." But he refused. He said, "You've got to put on your big-girl panties. You have to go in there like a boss. She's not good for the business, and you need to let her go." I eventually did it, and though I was upset with him at first, I'm grateful he pushed me out of my comfort zone because it was a necessary part of my role as CEO.

There have also been times when I've wanted to fire someone, but Melvin took their side. He's often more patient, giving people multiple chances, whereas I'm more of a "fool me once, shame on you; fool me twice, shame on me" type. Again, in those instances, we've had to come together and decide what's best for the business. And again, perfection doesn't exist here. Sometimes that worked; other times, not so much.

For example, we had another employee who was challenging to work with. Melvin, with his patient nature, took the time to mentor her and give her experience. We both believe in giving people opportunities, but I feel people need to meet us halfway. If they don't, I lose patience quickly. I've seen people take advice, ask questions, gain knowledge, then do nothing with it. With this employee, Melvin kept giving her advice, but she wasn't following through. She clashed with nearly everyone she worked with, which delayed projects and made things harder for us. Melvin had to step in and mediate the conflicts she created each time, and I'd think, *How long are you going to keep doing this?* It was now my turn to tell him to let her go. He was resistant.

While I will get frustrated if I feel like he's not listening to me, nine times out of ten that's not what is happening. He always says, "I listen to you. I take mental notes, but I also see the bigger picture. Sometimes it's faster to mediate and get the job done than to find a replacement and train someone new." In the end, though, this person ended up turning on us. I was right (of course). But I've also learned that even when or if I'm right, sometimes I need to step back. It's important to offer input, but also to let your partner have the agency to reach conclusions on their own.

—

We've also faced similar challenges with boundaries when it comes to how we work with the opposite sex. I've shared how secure Melvin is when he sees me taking pictures with or working alongside men. I've had to work on having that same security when it comes to women in our business. Obviously, we work in an industry full of beautiful Black women, many of whom are—how do I put this?—fairly assertive. My husband and I built this business together, so there are times when we need to be mindful of boundaries with certain women. I've had conversations with Melvin about this, as he's naturally friendly and extroverted—that's just his personality with everyone. I've reminded him that sometimes people might misinterpret his friendliness and gregarious nature as flirtatiousness. It's not that he's being flirtatious, but there are broken individuals out there who might take his friendliness and let it feed into their own issues, potentially setting him up for a false accusation.

So for us, trust is key. I have to trust my husband, and he has to trust me. He has never given me any reason to believe he'd do anything to harm our marriage, but we both know that it's still necessary to be mindful of how we interact with others. While there haven't been many instances where women have blatantly tried to come between us, there have been a few that made me side-eye and think, *What are you doing? You're getting a little too friendly.* The good thing is, we talk about it openly. He even tells me if someone slides into his DMs.

I've always told Melvin that we need to keep our personal and professional lives separate, but intertwined enough to remain connected. The trust we have for each other gives us both the confidence to travel and work independently. That said, when we're at a networking event or business function solo, we're careful about who we interact with and how. He has traveled with women for business, and I've done the same with men. I travel with my photographer, who's a man. We've been out, just the two of us, but my husband trusts that this is a professional relationship, and I'm not going to do anything to jeopardize my marriage or family. The photographer and I have even stayed at the same hotel while traveling, but, again, my husband trusts me completely. He doesn't question or accuse me. He's never once asked, "Were you really traveling with that man alone?" And whether it's him on the road or me, we're probably going to be on the phone all night anyway until we fall asleep. The point is, we can never let jealousy or insecurity get in the way. Now, granted, if I'm honest, Melvin might be slightly more secure than I am. I'm known to give a side-eye if a woman gets too close. But there's still a certain level of self-security you need in order to be okay with your partner traveling with the opposite sex. You can trust them, but if you're insecure, that trust will only go so far before your mind starts making up stories about what might be happening. That's why checking in with each other regularly, especially when we're apart—though it seems like a small thing—is something that keeps us connected and those stories at bay.

Another rule we've implemented is that we don't give our phone numbers to people we don't know of the opposite sex. We give people our assistants' email. Why? Well, because people can be slick. For instance, I once met a guy at a networking event who approached me and said, "I love what you're doing. I like what you and your husband have going on. I work with so-and-so," and he started name-dropping. Then he said, "I'd love to work with you both and see how I can help leverage or scale your careers. Do you mind if I get your number so we can connect?" At that point, my friend who was with me stepped in and said, "You can take my number. I'll connect with you on behalf of her and Melvin." I could tell he was a bit put off by that, but again, that's the boundary we've set.

I know some people will take issue with this rule of not taking the number of someone of the opposite sex. They will say, "If you trust him, why do that?" or "That feels very antiquated." That's okay. The one thing I've come to understand is that every couple has to do what works for them. This is what works for us. They are simple rules, but ones that help us avoid misunderstandings and stay on the same page. Every single boundary we set helps us protect our relationship while still growing our business. We trust our instincts and each other's judgment. If either of us feels uncomfortable with someone, we talk about it openly. That communication is what keeps us strong.

There was a situation where a woman I knew reached out to Melvin about a new project he was working on. She got his information from someone else and contacted him, saying, "I see what you're doing. I'm doing social media marketing, so if you ever need my services, please feel free to reach out." She left her phone number and contact information, and I was like, *What?*

He showed me the email, and I couldn't help but think, *You have a wife who built a business on social media and has experience with marketing. What do you need her help for?* This person had no real experience, hadn't built anything notable on social media, so why reach out like that? Sure, maybe she was just trying to get her hustle on. But I knew her. She knew me. It was strange that she didn't approach me first and say, "Hey, sis, I know you're busy. Does Melvin need any help?" But my main point is that Melvin and I have the kind of relationship where he shows me those messages. And he did exactly that. He showed me her email, and I made a mental note of that person. If or when I see her, I'll remain kind, but I'm still also asking myself, *What's your true motive? Why do you need a one-on-one meeting with him? What's your goal here?* We provide each other safety within our relationship because we know we're going to talk about everything. We will give each other a heads-up about people who might be manipulative, even if we're not sure yet. That way, we both know how to respond.

It's incredibly important for couples to trust their partner's intentions. For us, we trust that each of us has a personal conviction by God to maintain an honest and faithful marriage. As my husband always tells me, "If anything, I'm personally convicted by God first. Yeah, I'm scared of you, but I fear God too."

Trust is essential in our relationship. But even more than trust, we have security. We know that people can be manipulative, so we try to stay vigilant. We openly discuss these issues with each other and come up with solutions *before* they become a problem. We've seen other couples struggle with security, and I'm grateful that we've built a foundation of mutual respect and honesty. Maintaining a united front has allowed us to focus on our mission without forgetting what really matters. Again, it's always God, family, and business—in that order.

I think ultimately Melvin and I try to remind ourselves of who we were before Mielle. Not the teenagers, per se, but the man and woman who kept their eyes on each other and our family. Mielle is just an asset. Yes, it's something that we've built together, but it's not who we are, and it doesn't define our marriage. It doesn't define us as parents. It doesn't define us as human beings. It is simply something we do to make a living for our household and build our legacy. What matters most is what and who we see when we look at each other. When we search the eyes of our children.

Looking back, I'm grateful for the challenges we've faced in our marriage and partnership. Beyond the business, it's forced us to grow, both as individuals and as a couple. We've had to adapt to the complexities of running a business while keeping our relationship strong. Even when things were tight, and we didn't know if we'd make it, we constantly reminded ourselves to keep the main thing the main thing. I want that for you no matter what kind of partnership you have or even if you are still working on one. Never forget what matters most. It won't always be easy to navigate another person's evolution, but it's worth it. As long as you keep God at the center and make love a priority, you can face anything with those you love.

QUESTIONS FOR REFLECTION

- Think about how you and your partner or close relationships have evolved over time. What adjustments can you make to better support each other's journey and continue to grow together?
- Reflect on areas where outside influences may be impacting your connection with your partner or loved ones. How can setting or reinforcing boundaries help you maintain focus on what truly matters to you?

16

Living a Bigger Life

Guiding Principle:
Keep service ever in mind.

IT'S FUNNY TO THINK ABOUT WHERE I STARTED.
Growing up, I never imagined I would be here, that I would have this kind of influence and success. If you had told that little girl staring at the kiddie perm boxes longingly, or the teenager running around the South Side of Chicago that one day I would be the CEO of a multimillion-dollar company, I probably would have laughed. Back then, I thought the only way to make it big was to be a singer like Michael Jackson. But it didn't happen that way. I didn't need to be an entertainer to have this life. God had other plans for me, and I'm so grateful He did. It just goes to show that you don't have to follow the traditional path to success. Sometimes it's the unexpected detours that lead you to where you're meant to be.

Luke 12:48 says, "To whom much is given, from him much will be required" (NKJV). This is something I've chosen to live by in this season of my life. Yet, admittedly, it can be challenging to do so while navigating newfound wealth, access, and status. Even more so when trying to prioritize spiritual and family values. I've had to learn, sometimes the hard way, how to manage the blessings I've been given. It's been a journey of learning to balance my spiritual values with the demands of business. Of staying grounded even as my life transforms in ways I never would have believed before.

One of the most important takeaways I've had on this journey is the necessity of having an identity that goes beyond my business. Mielle is a huge part of my life, but it's not all that I am. I am a child of God first, so my identity is rooted in my faith, my relationship with God. I'm a wife and a mother second. So my identity is grounded in the nurture and care I give my family. I am a businesswoman *after* all that. And I now know that if I ever forget that order, I will be setting myself up for trouble. Everything I've achieved with Mielle is because of God's grace, but it wasn't because I was something special or different from you. My vision was just different. So every day, I try to live my life in a way that reflects that awareness. Because, really, none of the trappings of business success matter. How you live your life, how you treat people, the mark you leave on this earth when you're no longer here—*that's* what matters. You can't take any of this stuff with you. And as quickly as you achieve it, you can lose it. So I can't let any of this define me.

> How you live your life, how you treat people, the mark you leave on this earth when you're no longer here—*that's* what matters.

———

It can be tempting to let success feed your ego. To start thinking you're untouchable because of what you've achieved. But I've always believed that success doesn't change who you are; it just amplifies it. If you were a humble person before, success will generally make you even more so.

If you were generous before, success will give you the opportunity to be even more generous. On the other hand, if you were arrogant, if you looked down on others, success will only make those traits more visible. Sure, there may be exceptions to this, but it's been mostly true in my observation. The people I've met who are money hungry before their ventures take off usually end up staying money hungry afterward. And sadly, it is that money-over-everything mentality that becomes their downfall.

Melvin and I certainly wanted monetary success, but when we started Mielle, that wasn't the sole focus. We never got into this because we were chasing money. We enjoy money. We respect it. But we don't idolize it. We simply wanted to chase purpose. That was what fulfilling this dream meant to us. In fact, that became a kind of mantra for us: We don't chase dollars; we chase purpose. Even now, with all the influence and resources we have, it's still not about the money. We know for sure that when you walk in your purpose, the provision is a given.

But when I think about what money has done for us, maybe even *to* us, I can't help but consider how it has changed the way people treat me. It's a surreal thing to realize that access shifts how you can move in the world. That is something I'm still getting used to. I'll never forget the first time someone asked me for a selfie in public. It was such a strange feeling, realizing that people saw me as someone worth admiring, someone they wanted to capture a moment with. It's flattering, of course, but it can also be overwhelming. There are days when I just want to blend in and be anonymous. But I know that this is part of the territory, and I try to handle it with grace. Those moments are a reminder of how far I've come, of how much God has blessed me.

There are times when it moves beyond discomfort to a kind of intrusiveness. It can be frustrating when I'm at church, trying to worship, and someone comes up asking for a picture. I'll still take the photo because I know it means something to them, but I have to figure out what that boundary looks like. Church is a place I go to connect with God, to find peace and clarity, and it's hard when I have to switch gears and put on my public face. But even then, I never want to be unkind. I want to treat people with respect and warmth, no matter the circumstances, because I know that's what God has called me to do. The fame, the money—none of it matters if you don't have joy and peace in your heart. It certainly doesn't matter if that joy and peace doesn't reveal itself in how you interact with others. It is a true indication that a person is happy and well when they can find a way to serve others while still retaining the important parts of themselves. The parts that matter.

The catch? Only God can give us that. The joy and peace we are looking for comes from Him. Unfortunately, I've seen people who have all the money in the world but are still unhappy. They're empty inside because they don't have that connection with God. They don't have a sense of purpose beyond their bank account. You hear all the time about people with ridiculous amounts of money who die by suicide. Their souls were in turmoil and money couldn't save them.

I'm a realist. Money and the access that comes with it can absolutely make life easier. It can open doors and provide opportunities one might not have otherwise had. But it can't fill the void in our souls. I never want to idolize the success or wealth I've been given. God is a jealous God, and I know that if I put anything above Him, then that's akin to worship. I don't worship the blessings. I worship the One who gave them to me.

There was a moment recently that really drove this idea of having perspective home for me. I was going through an old journal and came across something I had written years ago. It was a vision I had for Mielle, a dream I had almost forgotten about. (Yes, just like the time I wrote my intentions about P&G. As you can see, this tends to happen to me quite a bit.) Seeing those words again gave me chills. It was like God was reminding me that He was the one orchestrating all of this. I might have done the work, but He was the one guiding my steps. That realization filled me with a sense of awe and gratitude. And now as I look to the future, I know that there is still so much I am being called to do.

Mielle was created from a place of pain and grief, but God has lifted up this brand for His glory. That wasn't me. I didn't do that. Melvin didn't do it. It's all God. There are a few people out there—yes, I'm talking about you, Day 1 Mavens and Mavericks—who have watched the entire ride. They saw the beginning struggles. They watched us in the middle, trying to figure out how to grow. And now they are experiencing the other side, the blessing, with us. Their comments always bless my heart: "I see what God has done for you, and that's given me so much more hope."

That's part of why I wanted to write this book. I see it as a gift to my community, a way to share the lessons I've learned and to hopefully inspire others to dream. There are too many dreams in the graveyard. Too many people have died with their dream in their heart. Don't let that be you.

———

More than anything I want you to see God's glory in my story, and maybe then you'll see His in yours. No matter where you come from, no matter what obstacles you face, you can achieve greatness. I want you to feel a spark of inspiration and know that if you keep pushing, if you keep believing, you can make those dreams a reality. No, it might not happen overnight. It might take five or ten or twenty years. But remember what I said at the very beginning: With God, it's always possible. His timing is always the right timing.

What I am saying is, You have the power to shape your future. And if you fail, guess what? You tried. If people talk about you? They're only talking about you because they also have a dream but are too scared to chase it. As Toni Morrison once said, failure is just information; it's a stepping stone to something greater.[1] And failure is also extremely relative, right? If you have a billion-dollar idea, why not pursue it? If you fail and only make a hundred million dollars, will you really be that mad? But you'll never have that opportunity if you don't pursue the billion-dollar idea. I've failed plenty of times in my life, and each failure has taught me something valuable. It's given me the tools I need to keep growing.

Do you know what the biggest and most impactful tool is? Community.

No one achieves success on their own. I can talk about naysayers and critics all day long because that's my experience, but I know I wouldn't be where I am today without the support of so many people who believed in me when no one else did. And now it's time for me to give back to them and others. It's time for me to serve.

That's really the bottom line, isn't it? The great Shirley Chisholm is believed to have said, "Service is the rent you pay for your room on this earth." My success and that of Mielle Organics wouldn't matter a single iota to the God who owns everything if it was not going to be used to prioritize serving my community. The only way to evolve as a person or business is to not just aim for a singular, personal goal but to always keep the flourishing of one's own community in the bigger picture. That community might mean your family. For me, that's always in the forefront of my mind. My youngest daughter dreams of owning her own farm, and I love that she has the freedom to imagine a life that's uniquely hers. I will support her dream in any way I can. But beyond family, our service might be needed in a much larger context.

This is part of why Melvin and I started MJR Ventures. We want to pay it forward, not just to our children and family, but to the next generation of Black entrepreneurs. We want to be the ones who believe in them, who give them a chance to succeed. Again, money is a secondary benefit. It's about making a difference. We want to change the narrative and normalize Black success. In this rapidly shifting world, it's easy to get caught up in the glam and chaos and lose sight of what's important. But I know that as long as I keep my eyes on God, as long as I stay true to my values, I'll be able to handle whatever comes my way. I want others to know that they can do the same.

So here's the charge: Dream big, friend. Stay adaptable and forward-looking, but never forget to cherish the present moment. Pursue your passions without apology. Then use whatever resources and influence you acquire to make a positive impact on the world.

The lessons of my life can be summed up in this way: Never forget where you come from, but know that with God, there's always more to come. More love, more joy, more abundance is yours. You just have to go get it.

QUESTIONS FOR REFLECTION

- What dreams or visions do you hold that could make a lasting impact on the world? Think about how you can take steps toward realizing these dreams.
- How do you currently use your influence and resources to serve your community or those around you? Consider specific ways you can give back or support others who are on their own journey.

Acknowledgments

THIS BOOK IS A LIVING TESTAMENT TO THE EXTRAOR-
dinary people, moments, and lessons that have shaped, guided, and uplifted me. It is not just my story but a celebration of the lives and spirits that have touched mine in profound ways.

First and foremost, I dedicate this book to my son, my angel, Milan Jordan Rodriguez. Milan, your time with us was brief, but your impact is infinite. You gave my life deeper purpose, and your presence brought clarity to my journey. You touched our family and the world in ways that words cannot fully capture. You are our guardian angel, watching over us with love and light. I am forever grateful for the gift of your life and the inspiration you have given me to walk boldly in my purpose. This work, this story, and every step I take are for you and because of you.

To my husband, Melvin Rodriguez—my partner, my king, and my greatest supporter—this book is as much yours as it is mine. Thank you for being my rock during the darkest of times, for pushing me when I wanted to give up, and for constantly reminding me of my strength. Your unwavering belief in me has carried me through every obstacle. You are my cheerleader, my confidant, and my partner in every sense of the word. Thank you for supporting me in building Mielle, for being my partner in raising our children, and for always celebrating my light. I couldn't have done any of this without your love, patience, and encouragement.

To my daughters, Mia and Mackenzie—my heart, my joy, and my legacy—you are the reason for everything I do. Thank you for sharing your mommy with the world and for your endless love and understanding. Every late night, every sacrifice, and every dream I have pursued has been for you and the generations that will come after you. I pray you always remember that through Christ, you can do all things. Let this journey be a testament to the power of faith, hard work, and perseverance. You are my *why*, and I love you both beyond measure.

To my mom, your sacrifices laid the foundation of everything I have accomplished. You raised my brother and me with strength, resilience, and an abundance of love, even when the odds were stacked against you. Your courage and selflessness taught me to dream big and never give up, no matter the circumstances. I hope you see now that all your sacrifices, sleepless nights, and emotional endurance were not in vain. You gave us the tools to thrive, and I pray you now feel the peace and joy you so deeply deserve. It's your time to rest, to bask in the fruits of your labor, and to live every day as if you're on vacation—you've earned it.

To my dad, thank you for encouraging me to share my story and for inspiring me to find strength in my truth. Your words—that my story could help someone else—gave me the courage to be vulnerable and open. I pray this book honors that vision and brings hope to those facing challenges similar to what I've overcome. Your belief in the power of storytelling has meant everything to me, and I carry your wisdom with me always.

To my father-in-law, Melvin Gayles—thank you for stepping in when we needed you most. From driving Mielle trucks across the country when we couldn't afford shipping to helping us with our children, your generosity and support have been a blessing to our family. Your love and willingness to go above and beyond have been invaluable to our journey.

To my mentor Germaine Bolds Leftridge—thank you for being

more than a guide. You've been a fairy godmother, a friend, and a constant source of wisdom and encouragement. Your belief in me and my vision has been a guiding light throughout this journey. Thank you for walking with me, believing in me, and mentoring me with such grace and care.

To the trailblazers who paved the way—Madam C. J. Walker, Lisa Price, Richelieu Dennis, and so many others—you have shown us what is possible. Your courage, innovation, and determination have been an inspiration to me and countless others. Thank you for opening doors and showing us how to dream bigger.

To Richelieu Dennis—thank you for your mentorship, your friendship, and your unwavering support. Your belief in us through the New Voices Fund, especially when others said no, was transformative. Your encouragement gave us the opportunity to grow and succeed in ways we never thought possible.

To our partners at Berkshire Partners—thank you for believing in our vision and taking a chance on us. Your investment in us, not just as a business but as people, has been pivotal to our success.

To our partners at P&G—thank you for believing in Mielle and for helping us scale to heights I once only dreamed of. This partnership has been a dream realized, and your support has allowed us to achieve extraordinary things.

To my writer, Tracey Lewis-Giggetts—thank you for your incredible patience, insight, and skill in helping me bring this story to life. This book was more than a project; it was a journey of reflection and healing, and you guided me through it with such care. Your ability to capture my thoughts and emotions has been a true gift.

To my agent, Rebecca, and Albert—thank you for seeing the vision and believing in the power of this story. Your dedication and faith in me have made this possible.

To Kyle Olund, Lauren Bridges, and the entire W Publishing/ HarperCollins Christian team—thank you for believing in me and being willing to put this book out into the world. I'm so grateful that you've come alongside me to ensure that the story is told, and God gets the glory.

To Eula—thank you for your encouragement, your belief in me, and your unwavering support. You gave me the confidence to move forward and share my journey with the world.

To everyone who has been part of the Mielle journey—from packing boxes in the early days to managing marketing, finance, operations, and everything in between—thank you. Every role you've played, every effort you've made, has contributed to building this dream into a reality.

To our incredible community of Mavens and Mavericks—your support has been the heartbeat of this brand. Every bottle you purchased, every event you attended, every word of encouragement you shared—it has all mattered. You are part of this legacy, and I am endlessly grateful for you.

To my prayer warriors—you know who you are. Thank you for standing with me in faith through every high and every low. Your prayers have sustained me, your love has uplifted me, and your guidance has taught me to build my spiritual muscle. I am forever grateful for your unwavering presence in my life.

Finally, to everyone who has believed in me, supported me, and walked this journey with me—this book is as much yours as it is mine. Whether through advice, encouragement, or simply showing up when I needed you most, your impact has left an indelible mark on my heart.

This book is for all of you. It is a reflection of faith, perseverance, and the transformative power of love and community. Thank you for being part of this journey and for believing in the beauty of what we could create together.

Notes

INTRODUCTION: SEEK GOD FIRST

1. See Maria Shriver's podcast series "Architects of Change," www.mariashriver
.com/aoc.

CHAPTER 1: FINDING TRUE NORTH ON THE SOUTH SIDE

1. "Maya Angelou: In Her Own Words," BBC News, May 28, 2014,
https://www.bbc.com/news/world-us-canada-27610770.

CHAPTER 2: YOU ARE MORE THAN WHAT YOU'VE SEEN

1. Bud Billiken Parade, Chicago Defender Charities, Inc., https://www
.budbillikenparade.org/.

CHAPTER 5: EMBRACING GOD'S PLAN IN THE PIVOT

1. T.D. Jakes, "Ignore the Turtles in Life," Facebook video, May 26, 2016,
https://www.facebook.com/watch/?v=843207382476523.
2. "Take the First Step in Faith. You Don't Have To See the Whole Staircase,
Just Take the First Step," Quote Investigator, April 18, 2019, https://
quoteinvestigator.com/2019/04/18/staircase/.

NOTES

CHAPTER 13: FINDING YOUR PEOPLE

1. Nedra Glover Tawwab, "Things to Remember About Boundaries," Nedra's Nuggets, Substack blog post, August 15, 2023, https://nedratawwab.substack.com/p/things-to-remember-about-boundaries.

CHAPTER 16: LIVING A BIGGER LIFE

1. Rebecca Sutton, "Toni Morrison: Write, Erase, Do It Over," NEA Arts no. 4 (2014), https://www.arts.gov/stories/magazine/2014/4/art-failure-importance-risk-and-experimentation/toni-morrison#:~:text=As%20a%20writer%2C%20a%20failure,That's%20rewriting%20and%20editing.

About the Author

MONIQUE RODRIGUEZ IS THE FOUNDER AND CEO OF
Mielle Organics, one of the fastest-growing hair care brands in the textured hair category. Previously a registered nurse, Monique shifted her career path after the tragic loss of her third child following a high-risk pregnancy. After this devastating event, Monique needed a creative outlet to help process her grief and turned to her original passion—hair care. She took to social media to share her journey of creating a healthy hair care regimen for textured hair, thus building a tight-knit online community of loyal and engaged women.

Her deeply personal documentation resonated with her followers, who would tune in daily for her hair care tips, as well as morning prayer moments. Monique's community kept requesting her homemade mixtures, and their demand to buy her hair care solutions served as the catalyst for her to launch Mielle Organics with her husband, Melvin. They launched in 2014 with one product, the Almond Mint Oil and immediately sold out of their entire inventory on the day of launch.

In addition to breaking glass ceilings and barriers for female and Black founders, notably securing the largest exit ever for a Black Female beauty founder, she is also a wife, mother of two girls, and a devout

Christian. She has dedicated her life to uplifting God's Kingdom and moving in His purpose. Monique continues to be a vessel and extol His mercy, goodness, and love.

Monique is committed to inspiring women around the world through her beauty solutions and business savvy. In 2023, she established Mielle Cares, the nonprofit arm of Mielle Organics, which champions the mental health and well–being of preteens and teenagers in underserved communities. She has been widely recognized in media publications, was featured on the cover of *Essence* alongside her husband, Melvin, and has appeared in outlets and on television shows such as Forbes.com, CNBC.com, *CBS*, *Tamron Hall Show*, and *The Steve Harvey Show*. Her journey serves as an inspiration to countless individuals, demonstrating the power of passion, perseverance, and community.